Unbounded Light

Unbounded Light

THE INWARD JOURNEY

15
Tales of
the Inner Light
from Ancient Scriptures,
First Person Accounts, and Modern Science
——— Compiled and Edited by ———

William E. Williams

NICOLAS-HAYS, INC.
York Beach, Maine

First published in 1992 by
Nicolas-Hays, Inc.
Box 612
York Beach, ME 03910

Distributed to the trade by
Samuel Weiser, Inc.
Box 612
York Beach, ME 03910

Library of Congress Cataloging-in-Publication Data
Williams, William E.
    Unbounded light : the inward journey / by William E.
Williams.
        p.   cm.
    Includes bibliographical references.
    1. Light--Religious aspects.   2. Consciousness--Religious
aspects.
    3. Inner Light.   I. Title.
    BL265.L5W55   1992
    291.4'2--dc20   92-1759
                                                              CIP
ISBN 0-89254-023-0
BJ

Cover photograph copyright © 1992 Dale O'Dell.
Used by kind permission.

Calligraphy by Ruth Schukman-Dakotas and Janice Ostrom

The Epilogue is from *Kundalini: The Evolutionary Energy in Man*, by
Gopi Krishna (Boston: Shambhala Publications, Inc., 1985), p. 250.
Copyright © 1967 Gopi Krishna.

Typeset in 11 point Palatino
Printed in the United States of America

The paper used in this publication meets the minimum requirements of the American National Standard for Permanence of Paper
for printed Library Materials Z39.48-1984.

Dedicated to
all who seek inward

Note: The stories presented in this book are abridgments of original works. Certain passages have been deleted and separate passages brought together. But the use of ellipses (. . .) has been generally avoided, since their inclusion would be so common and so repetitive as to be disruptive to the reading of the stories as here presented. Any reader who wishes to examine the original full version of any selection should consult the references provided.

Contents

Introduction ix

Part I: Scripture
1. Nachiketa's Wish 3
2. Original Mind 13
3. Baptism by Fire 25

Part II: First-Hand Accounts
4. The Confessions of St. Augustine 41
5. The Sutra of Hui-Neng 55
6. The Meccan Pilgrimage of Al-Ghazali 71
7. The Shekhinah 89
8. The Prayer of Quiet 105
9. The Master Shoemaker 125
10. The Journal of George Fox 139
11. At the Hermitage of Father Seraphim 159
12. The Himalayas Within 171

Part III: Science
13. Riding a Beam of Light in Modern Physics ... 189
14. The Light of Life 211
15. The Light of Death 225

Epilogue 241

Introduction

The fifteen stories in this anthology center around two great mysteries—light and consciousness. Both light and consciousness are basic to our experience of life, forever with us in every waking moment. They are so basic to the act of perception that we cannot fully separate ourselves from them in order to scrutinize them objectively. Science, which demands objectivity above all, struggles to provide definitions. Light, modern physics tells us, is "an electromagnetic wave disturbance of a frequency between 10^{14} and 10^{15} oscillations per second." But given such a definition, we are still tempted to ask: "Okay, but what *is* it?" As for consciousness, our present scientific understanding is virtually nil. "Science's biggest mystery," says modern day physicist Nick Herbert, "is the nature of consciousness. It's not that we possess bad or imperfect theories of human awareness; we simply have no such theories at all."[1]

Fortunately, our exploration of life's mysteries is not limited to the objective methodologies of science. Each one of us has our own subjective experience of being conscious. This immediately presents an alternative course to the scientific study of consciousness, and that is to simply see for ourselves—within. This course is, in fact, well-traveled and well-documented, although it has often been called the "secret path" since its findings are largely

---

[1]Nick Herbert, *Quantum Reality* (Garden City, NY: Doubleday, 1985), p. 249.

untranslatable into human language. The first documenta-
tion of the inner investigation of consciousness comes to
us symbolically from the world's ancient myths and leg-
ends. These stories are often best understood as allegories
of the spiritual path. The dangerous terrain that mytholog-
ical heroes traverse is none other than their own psyche,
and the boon they ultimately recover is true self-
knowledge.

When we gather the many stories of the inward
adventure, we find a curious phenomenon; we come
again to light. Light is easily the most universal and often-
mentioned aspect of higher consciousness experiences, a
light not seen by physical eyes, but perceived within. This
light is not only perceived, but identified with as a shining
self-awareness far beyond the limits of body and
personality—consciousness and light unbounded as one
timeless being. It is here in this personal, inward experience that the greatest understanding of life is achieved.

Each of the world's major religions has its tradition of
the inner light. When we compare the various sacred texts
on inner light from around the world, we find an unmis-
takable commonality. In fact, we might say we have found
a single tradition of the inner light, the differences being
only superficial ones of age, culture, and language. The
light is known by many names. It is *Vergo* in the ancient
Hindu Vedas, *Param Prakash* in the Ramayana, *Divya Jyoti*
in the Upanishads, *Amitabha* in the Mahayana Buddhist
scriptures, *Light* in the Bible, *Noor-e-Ilahi* in the Koran,
Shekinah in the Zohar, and *Chandna* in the Sikh scriptures.

Although the inner light tradition is a great common
denominator, it is also a great divider. Historically, claims
of higher consciousness experiences by the world's sages
and seers have been met with extreme scepticism, leading
to a certain dichotomy within religion: the *esoteric path* of
direct inward realization and the *exoteric path* of mainstream organized religion. This dichotomy is particularly

antagonistic in Western religions—Christianity, Judaism, and Islam. To cite just one of numerous examples, the 14th-century Catholic priest Meister Eckhart spoke openly about his direct spiritual experiences. His sermons, which contain such declarations as "If the soul is to know God, it must know him above time and outside of space"[2] brought upon him the official condemnation of Pope John XXII, who said Eckhart wished to know more than he should. Many of the stories in this anthology were written by seers who encountered similar difficulties.

Even today, the path toward higher consciousness is dark and controversial. The inner light is dismissed as mere hallucination by some modern-day neurophysicists, and it continues to provoke the charge of blasphemy from some fundamentalist religious quarters where it is equated with the dark side of the occult. Such controversy is not surprising, for the inner light is not easily revealed. It lies beyond ordinary time-space and beyond the grasp of the rational mind.

What is the truth of the inner light? Is it Eastern, or Western? Real, or imaginary? Is it forever beyond our reach, or our own true self? Is it a new-age tenet inconsistent with orthodox religion, or a universal, time-honored tradition? And how is it described by the men and women who have attained it? These are the questions that have prompted the compilation of this book.

The fifteen stories collected here are presented in chronological order and span the time from a thousand years before Christ through the present day. A great variety of culture is represented. The first three stories are compiled from the sacred texts of three major religions and represent the main scriptural basis for the inner light tradition. The rest are stories from the first-person per-

---

[2]Meister Eckhart, *Meister Eckhart: A Modern Translation*, trans. Raymond B. Blakney (New York: HarperCollins, 1941), p. 131.

spective, for the inner light is best described, not in holy books, but in the autobiographical accounts of men and women who have directly experienced it. Such accounts are abundant and diverse. In the stories gathered here, we hear from a highly educated Catholic bishop, but also from an unschooled German shoemaker; from a man who traveled widely and preached to thousands, but also from a hermit who took a vow of silence; from celibate renunciates, to people who led normal married lives. Each story tells of long personal struggle and ultimate illumination.

Finally, we turn to modern science to examine what physics, cosmology, biology, medicine, and thanatology (the study of death and dying) have to tell us about the inner light tradition.

Here now are the stories. Read them during a quiet time, two or three at a sitting. May they be a map for your own seeking.

PART I

SCRIPTURE

1

NACHIKETA'S WISH

अथ यदतः परो दिवो

ज्योतिर्दीप्यते विश्वतः पृष्ठेषु

सर्वतः पृष्ठेष्वनुत्तमेषूत्तमेषु

लोकेष्विदं वाव तद्यदिदम-

स्मिन्नन्तः

The light that shines above the heavens and
above this world, the light that shines in the
highest world, beyond which there are no others, that is the light that shines in the hearts of
men.

———The Chandogya Upanishad

♦ ♦ ♦

This first tale of the inner light is taken from the oldest written records of Hinduism. It is the adventure story of a young seeker of truth named Nachiketa. It was recorded as the Katha Upanishad, no one knows exactly when. But we do know that this story, and the other Upanishads, were passed down orally for generations, centuries before the invention of writing. Thus, this story well represents the most ancient origins of the inner light tradition. Nachiketa's story contains many of the universal elements of legend: a hero setting forth on adventure, the passage to an unknown higher kingdom, trials and tests, and the final boon of knowledge. The following version contains excerpts from the Katha Upanishad with some concluding instructions added from the Svetasvatara Upanishad.

♦ ♦ ♦

On a certain occasion Vajasrabasa, hoping for divine favor, performed a rite which required that he should give away all his possessions. He was careful, however, to sacrifice only his cattle, and of these only such as were useless—the old, the barren, the blind, and the lame. Observing this niggardliness, Nachiketa, his young son, thought to himself: "Surely a worshiper who dares bring such worthless gifts is doomed to utter darkness!" Thus reflecting, he came to his father, and cried:

"Father, I too belong to thee: to whom givest thou me?"

His father did not answer; but when Nachiketa asked the question again and yet again, he replied impatiently: "Thee I give to Death!"

Then Nachiketa thought to himself: "Of my father's many sons and disciples I am indeed the best, or at least of the middle rank, not the worst; but of what good am I to the King of Death?" Yet being determined to keep his father's word he said:

"Father, do not repent thy vow! Consider how it has been with those that have gone before, and how it will be with those that now live. Like corn, a man ripens and falls to the ground; like corn, he springs up again in his season."

Having thus spoken, the boy journeyed to the house of Death. But the god was not at home, and for three nights Nachiketa waited. When at length the King of Death returned, he was met by his servants, who said to him:

"A Brahmin, like to a flame of fire, entered thy house as guest, and thou wast not there. Therefore must a peace offering be made to him. With all accustomed rites, O King, thou must receive thy guest, for if a householder show not due hospitality to a Brahmin, he will lose what he most desires—the merits of his good deeds, his righteousness, his sons, and his cattle."

Then the King of Death approached Nachiketa and welcomed him with courteous words.

"O Brahmin," he said, "I salute thee. Thou art indeed a guest worthy of all reverence. Let, I pray thee, no harm befall me! Three nights hast thou passed in my house and hast not received my hospitality; ask of me, therefore, three boons—one for each night."

"O Death," replied Nachiketa, "so let it be. And as the first of these boons I ask that my father be not anxious about me, that his anger be appeased, and that when thou sendest me back to him, he recognize me and welcome me."

"By my will," declared Death, "thy father shall recognize thee and love thee as heretofore; and seeing thee again alive, he shall be tranquil of mind, and he shall sleep in peace."

Then said Nachiketa: "In heaven there is no fear at all. Thou, O Death, art not there, nor in that place does the thought of growing old make one tremble. There, free from hunger and from thirst, and far from the reach of sorrow, all rejoice and are glad. Thou knowest, O King, the fire sacrifice that leads to heaven. Teach me that sacrifice, for I am full of faith. This is my second wish."

Whereupon, consenting, Death taught the boy the fire sacrifice, and all the rites and ceremonies attending it. Nachiketa repeated all that he had learned, and Death, well pleased with him, said:

"I grant thee an extra boon. Henceforth shall this sacrifice be called the Nachiketa Sacrifice, after thy name. Choose now thy third boon."

And then Nachiketa considered within himself, and said:

"When a man dies, there is this doubt: Some say, he is; others say, he is not. Taught by thee, I would know the truth. This is my third wish."

"Nay," replied Death, "even the gods were once puzzled by this mystery. Subtle indeed is the truth regarding it, not easy to understand. Choose thou some other boon, O Nachiketa."

But Nachiketa would not be denied.

"Thou sayest, O Death, that even the gods were once puzzled by this mystery, and that it is not easy to understand. Surely there is no teacher better able to explain it than thou—and there is no other boon equal to this."

To which, trying Nachiketa again, the god replied:

"Ask for sons and grandsons who shall live a hundred years. Ask for cattle, elephants, horses, gold. Choose for thyself a mighty kingdom. Or if thou canst imagine aught better, ask for that—not for sweet pleasure only but for the power, beyond all thought, to taste their sweetness. Yea, verily, the supreme enjoyer will I make thee of every good thing. Celestial maidens, beautiful to behold, such indeed as were not meant for mortals—even these, together with their bright chariots and their musical instruments, will I give unto thee, to serve thee. But for the secret of death, O Nachiketa, do not ask!"

But Nachiketa stood fast, and said: "These things endure only till the morrow, O Destroyer of Life, and the pleasures they give wear out the senses. Keep thou therefore horses and chariots, keep dance and song, for thyself! How shall he desire wealth, O Death, who once has seen thy face? Nay, only the boon that I have chosen—that only do I ask. Having found out the society of the imperishable and the immortal, as in knowing thee I have done, how shall I, subject to decay and death, and knowing well the vanity of the flesh—how shall I wish for long life?

"Tell me, O King, the supreme secret regarding which men doubt. No other boon will I ask."

Whereupon the King of Death, well pleased at heart, began to teach Nachiketa the secret of immortality:

Both the good and the pleasant present themselves to men. The wise, having examined both, distinguish the one from the other. Far from each other, and leading to different ends, are ignorance and knowledge. Thee, O Nachiketa, I regard as one who aspires after knowledge.

To many it is not given to hear of the Self. Many, though they hear of it, do not understand it. Wonderful is he who speaks of it. Intelligent is he who learns of it. Blessed is he who, taught by a good teacher, is able to understand it.

The truth of the Self cannot be fully understood when taught by an ignorant man, for opinions regarding it, not founded in knowledge, vary one from another. Subtler than the subtlest is this Self, and beyond all logic. Taught by a teacher who knows the Self and Brahman [God] as one, a man leaves vain theory behind and attains to truth.

The awakening which thou hast known does not come through the intellect, but rather, in fullest measure, from the lips of the wise. Beloved Nachiketa, blessed, blessed art thou, because thou seekest the Eternal. Would that I had more pupils like thee!

The ancient, effulgent being, the indwelling Spirit, subtle, deep-hidden in the lotus of the heart, is hard to know. But the wise man, following the path of meditation, knows him and is freed alike from pleasure and from pain.

Smaller than the smallest, greater than the greatest, this Self forever dwells within the hearts of all. When a man is free from desire, his mind and senses purified, he beholds the glory of the Self and is without sorrow.

Though seated, he travels far; though at rest, he moves all things. Who but the purest of the pure can realize this Effulgent Being, who is joy and who is beyond joy.

Formless is he, though inhabiting form. In the midst of the fleeting he abides forever. All-pervading and supreme is the Self. The wise man, knowing him in his true nature, transcends all grief.

The Self is not known through study of the scriptures, nor through subtlety of the intellect, nor through much learning. But by him who longs for him is he known. Verily unto him does the Self reveal his true being.

This Brahman, this Self, deep-hidden in all beings, is not revealed to all; but to the seers, pure in heart, concentrated in mind—to them is he revealed. Arise! Awake! Approach the feet of the Master and know THAT. Like the sharp edge of a razor, the sages say, is the path. Narrow it is, and difficult to tread! Man looks toward what is without, and sees not what is within. Rare is he who, longing for immortality, shuts his eyes to what is without and beholds the Self.

To the Birthless, the light of whose consciousness forever shines, belongs the city of eleven gates [i.e., the human body]. He who meditates on the ruler of that city knows no more sorrow. He attains liberation, and for him there can no longer be birth or death. For the ruler of that city is the immortal Self.

The immortal Self is the sun shining in the sky, he is the breeze blowing in space, he is the fire burning on the altar, he is the guest dwelling in the house, he is in all men, he is in the gods, he is in the ether, he is wherever there is truth; he is the fish that is born in water, he is the plant that grows in the soil, he is the river that gushes from the mountain—he, the changeless reality, the illimitable!

He, the adorable one, seated in the heart, is the power that gives breath. Unto him all the senses do homage.

Then asked Nachiketa: "How, O King, shall I find this blissful Self, supreme, ineffable, who is attained by the wise? Does he shine by himself, or does he reflect another's light?"

Him the sun does not illumine, nor the moon, nor the stars, nor the lightning—nor, verily, fires kindled upon the earth. He is the one light that gives light to all. He shining, everything shines. None beholds him with the eyes, for he is without visible form. Yet in the heart is he revealed, through self-control and meditation. Those who know him become immortal. When all the senses are stilled, when the mind is at rest, when the intellect wavers not—that, say the wise, is the highest state.

Nachiketa, having learned from the god this knowledge and the whole process of yoga, was freed from impurities and from death, and was united with Brahman. Thus will it be with another also if he know the innermost Self.

To realize God, first control the outgoing senses and harness the mind. Then meditate upon the light in the heart of the fire—meditate, that is, upon pure consciousness as distinct from the ordinary consciousness of the intellect. Thus the Self, the Inner Reality, may be seen behind physical appearance.

Control your mind so that the Ultimate Reality, the self-luminous Lord, may be revealed. Strive earnestly for eternal bliss.

With the help of the mind and the intellect, keep the senses from attaching themselves to objects of pleasure. They will then be purified by the light of the Inner Reality, and that light will be revealed.

The wise control their minds, and unite their hearts with the infinite, the omniscient, the all-pervading Lord. Only discriminating souls practice spiritual disciplines. Great is the glory of the self-luminous being, the Inner Reality.

Control the vital force. Set fire to the Self within by the practice of meditation. Be drunk with the wine of divine love. Thus shall you reach perfection.

2

ORIGINAL MIND

*Yesam sambodhiyaṅgesu sammā cittam subhāvitam
ādānapatinissagge anupādāya ye ratā
khināsavā jutimanto te loke parinibbutā.*

Those whose minds are well fixed upon the elements of enlightenment, who, without hankering after anything, glory in renunciation, whose biases are extinguished, who are full of light, they indeed have attained the bliss of Nirvana in this very world.

———Buddha
The Dhammapada

♦ ♦ ♦

It is estimated that there exist today nearly 600 sects of Buddhism. The number of Buddhist scriptures is also staggering—more than ten thousand, written in a dozen languages over a period of fifteen hundred years. Ironically, this overabundance of scripture centers around a single man who advised his immediate followers to rely upon personal experience over dogma and written scripture. This man was Prince Siddhartha Gautama of Kapilavatthu.

The accounts of Siddhartha's life are plentiful, but unreliable. There are numerous renditions, but since the first of these was not reduced to writing until 400 years after Siddhartha's passing, we can be sure that historical accuracy and pure legend mingle freely in these accounts. But certain basic facts of Siddhartha's life are generally agreed upon, as follows. He was born around 563 B.C., the only son of the ruler of Kapilavatthu, a small principality near the Himalayas. He was raised amid extreme luxury. He married young and fathered a son. But at age 29, he abandoned his family and kingdom and adopted the life of a wandering ascetic. After studying with the leading philosophers of the day, he rejected philosophy. After practicing severe self-mortification, he rejected asceticism. Then, at the age of 35, in solitary, silent introspection, he realized his goal and attained enlightenment. The remainder of his life was spent in spreading his message of the eightfold path to Nirvana. He gained a vast following during his lifetime and died at age 80.

Buddha's foremost teaching is, of course, the concept of Nirvana. But because Nirvana is a state of mind beyond all thought-conception, the Buddha refused to offer any concrete descriptions of it, usually saying only that it is "neither this, nor that." He was equally averse to commenting on the many abstruse philosophies popular in his time, and was also reluctant to divulge the details of his own enlightenment. He insisted rather on a philosophy that was simply stated and easy to understand, a practical way of life which would lead the aspirant to his or her own personal attainment of Nirvana. However, the Buddha was frequently pressed to offer more revealing descriptions of enlightenment and there do exist recorded attempts to put into words the inner workings of Nirvana. In time, a branch of Buddhism developed around the tradition of the *Amitabha,* the inner Buddha of boundless light (from *amita,* infinite, and *abha,* ray of light). But the inner light tradition in Buddhism is not limited to any one particular scripture or school; rather, it is fundamental to the *experience* of the Buddha. As he proclaims in the famous sermon at Benares, "Among doctrines unheard, in me sight and knowledge arose, wisdom arose, knowledge arose, light arose."[1] The following tale of the inner light is a compilation of excerpts from nearly a dozen well-known Buddhist scriptures.

♦   ♦   ♦

"I, too, monks, before my enlightenment, I myself being subject to birth, sought only that which is subject to birth. I myself being subject to old age, illness, death, grief, and mental impurity sought only for that which is subject to old age, illness, death, grief, and mental impurity. During that time, monks, I was delicately nurtured, exceedingly delicately nurtured. For instance, in my father's house, lotus pools were made thus, one of blue lotuses, one of red, another of white lotuses, just for my benefit. No sandlewood powder did I use that was not of Kasi, of Kasi cloth was my turban made, of Kasi cloth was my jacket,

---

[1] E. A. Burtt, *The Teachings of the Compassionate Buddha* (New York: NAL, 1982), p. 30.

my tunic, and my cloak. By night and day a white canopy
was held over me, lest cold or heat, dust or chaff or dew
should touch me. Moreover I had three palaces: one for
the winter, one for summer, and one for the rainy season.
In the four months of the rain, I was waited upon by
minstrels, women all of them. I came not down from my
palace in those months.

"Now monks, it occurred to me: What if I, myself,
being subject to birth, old age, illness, etc., and knowing
the danger in that which is subject to birth, should seek for
Nirvana which is not characterized by birth, is incomparable and is safety from bondage? Monks, that very I, at a
time even when I was young with jet black hair, endowed
with handsome youthfulness and early life, shaved off my
hair and beard, put on the yellow garments and went
forth from the household life to the homeless state against
the wish of my parents.

"That I, monks, while seeking for what was good and
searching for the incomparable noble state of peace, and
while traveling in Magadha by stages, came to the village
of Senani at Uruvela. There I saw a pleasant and delightful
forest grove with a flowing river of clear water, a pleasant
and delightful ford and a village near by for procuring
food. Monks, I sat down at that very spot thinking: This is
a most suitable place for spiritual exertion. Monks, being
myself subject to birth, while seeking for Nirvana which is
not characterized by birth, is incomparable and is safety
from bondage, I attained the state of Nirvana which is not
characterized by birth, is incomparable and is safety from
bondage.

"There is, monks, a condition wherein there is neither
earth, nor water, nor fire, nor air, nor the sphere of infinite
space, nor the sphere of infinite consciousness, nor the
sphere of the void, nor the sphere of neither perception
nor non-perception: where there is no 'this world' and no
'world beyond': where there is no moon and no sun. That

condition, monks, do I call neither a coming nor a going nor a standing still nor a falling away nor a rising up; but it is without fixity, without mobility, without basis. That is the end of suffering.

"There are two extremes, O monks, which a holy man should avoid—the habitual practice of self-indulgence, which is vulgar and profitless, and the habitual practice of self-mortification, which is painful and equally profitless. There is a middle path, O monks, a path which opens the eyes, and bestows understanding, which leads to peace of mind, to the higher wisdom, to full enlightenment, to Nirvana. Verily! it is the noble eightfold path; that is to say: right views, right aspirations, right speech, right conduct, right livlihood, right effort, right mindfulness, and right contemplation. Now this, O monks, is the noble truth concerning the end of suffering.

"What now, is right contemplation? Detached from sensual objects, detached from evil things, the disciple enters into the first level of contemplation, which is accompanied by thought-conception and discursive thinking, is born of detachment and filled with rapture and joy. After the subsiding of thought-conception and discursive thinking, and by gaining tranquility and one-pointedness of mind, he enters into a state free from thought-conception and discursive thinking, the second level of contemplation, which is born of concentration and filled with rapture and joy. After the fading away of rapture, he dwells in equanimity, being mindful and clearly conscious; and he experiences in his person that ease which the Noble Ones speak of when they say: 'Happy lives the man of equanimity and attentive mind.' He enters the third level of contemplation. After having given up pleasure and pain, and through the disappearance of the joy and grief which he had previously, he enters into a state beyond pleasure and pain, into the fourth level of contemplation, a state of pure equanimity and clear mindfulness.

This is called right contemplation. This is the noble truth of the path leading to the end of suffering."

Now it occurred to the venerable Malunkyaputta, a would-be disciple, that there were many problems which the Blessed One refused to elucidate—for example, whether or not the world is eternal, whether the soul is one thing and the body another, and whether the saint exists after death. "These," said Malunkyaputta to himself, "the Blessed One does not elucidate to me, and that fact does not please me. Therefore I will go to the Blessed One and inquire of him. If he will elucidate these problems to me, I shall join his order, and if not, then I shall abandon religious training and return to the lower life of a layman."

So the venerable Malunkyaputta arose at eventide from his seclusion, and drew near to where the Blessed One was; and having drawn near and greeted the Blessed One, he sat down respectfully at one side. And seated respectfully at one side, the venerable Malunkyaputta spoke to the Blessed One as follows:

"If the Blessed One knows that the world is eternal, let the Blessed One elucidate to me that the world is eternal; if the Blessed One knows that the world is not eternal, let the Blessed One elucidate to me that the world is not eternal . . . "

"Pray, Malunkyaputta, did I ever say to you, 'Come, Malunkyaputta, lead the religious life under me, and I will elucidate to you such matters'?"

"Nay, verily, Reverend Sir."

"Your attitude is like that of a man who has been wounded by an arrow thickly smeared with poison, and when his friends procure for him a physician or surgeon, he says, 'I will not have this arrow taken out until I have learnt whether the arrow which wounded me was an ordinary arrow, or a claw-headed arrow, or an iron arrow, or a calf-tooth arrow.' That man would die, Malunkyaputta, before he could learn any of these things. In exactly the same way, Malunkyaputta, anyone who should say, 'I will not lead the religious life under the Blessed One until the Blessed One elucidates so and so and so forth, that person would die before the elucidation could be made to him.

"The religious life, Malunkyaputta, does not depend on the dogma that the world is eternal; nor does the religious life, Malunkyaputta, depend on the dogma that the world is not eternal. No matter what the dogma, there still remain birth, old age, death, sorrow, lamentation, misery, grief, and despair. And it is against these here on earth that I prescribe the religious life. The origin of suffering and the end of suffering and the path leading to the end of suffering I have elucidated, because this does profit; it has to do with the fundamentals of religion; it tends to aversion, absence of passion, cessation, quiescence, knowledge, supreme wisdom, and Nirvana."

"Venerable one, it is said that Nirvana is neither in the past, nor in the future, nor in the present, that it is not produced, nor is it produced. Then say a man rightly practices, and realizes Nirvana: does he realize something already produced, or does he produce it first and then realize it?"

"He neither realizes something already produced, nor does he produce it first and then realize it. And yet the realm of Nirvana exists, that he may rightly practice, and realize it."

"Venerable one, do not explain the question by making it dark; explain it by making it open and unconcealed. Willingly heap upon me all that you have been taught, for people are bewildered and perplexed, and full of doubt. Destroy this dagger in my heart."

"The realm of Nirvana exists, calm and blissful and exalted. And a man may rightly practice, and know conditioned things according to the teachings of the Buddha, and realize Nirvana with his wisdom.

"Our original Buddha-nature is, in all truth, nothing which can be apprehended. It is void, omnipresent, silent, pure; it is glorious and mysterious peacefulness, and that is all which can be said. You yourself must awake to it, fathoming its depths. That which is before you is it in all its entirety and with nothing whatsoever lacking. Even if you go through all the stages of a Bodhisattva's progress towards Buddhahood, stage by stage, when at last, by a single flash of thought, you attain to full realization, you will only be realizing your original Buddha-nature and by all the foregoing stages you will not have added a single thing to it.

"This pure mind, the source of everything, shines on all with the brilliance of its own perfection, but the people of the world do not awake to it, regarding only that which sees, hears, feels, and knows as mind. Because their understanding is veiled by their own sight, hearing, feeling, and knowledge, they do not perceive the spiritual brilliance of the original substance. If they could only eliminate all analytic thinking in a flash, that original substance would manifest itself like the sun ascending through the void and illuminating the whole universe without hindrance or bounds.

"As earnest disciples go on trying to advance on the path that leads to full realization, there is one danger against which they must be on their guard. Disciples may not appreciate that the mind-system, because of its accumulated habit-energy, goes on functioning, more or less unconsciously, as long as they live. They may sometimes think that they can expedite the attainment of their goal of tranquillization by entirely suppressing the activities of the mind-system. This is a mistake, for even if the activities of the mind are suppressed, the mind will still go on functioning because the seeds of habit-energy will still remain in it. The true functioning of the mind is very subtle and difficult to be understood by young disciples.

They do not know that Nirvana is Universal Mind in its purity. Some conceive Nirvana to be a state where there is no recollection of the past or present, just as when a lamp is extinguished, or when a seed is burnt, or when a fire goes out; because then there is the cessation of all the substrate, which is explained by the philosophers as the non-rising of discrimination. But this is not Nirvana, because Nirvana does not consist in simple annihilation and vacuity.

"The truth of Noble Wisdom is beyond the reasoning knowledge of the philosophers as well as being beyond the understanding of ordinary disciples and masters; and is realizable only within the inmost consciousness. People grasping their own shadows of discrimination become attached to this thing and that thing and failing to abandon dualism they go on forever discriminating and thus never attain tranquillity. By tranquillity is meant Oneness, and Oneness gives birth to the highest Samadhi which is gained by entering into the realm of Noble Wisdom that is realizable only within one's inmost consciousness. When appearances and names are put away and all discrimination ceases, that which remains is the true and essential nature of things and, as nothing can be predicated as to the nature of essence, it is called the 'Suchness' of Reality. This universal, undifferentiated, inscrutable, 'Suchness' is the only Reality but it is variously characterized as Truth, Mind-essence, Transcendental Intelligence, Noble Wisdom, etc.

"When you understand well the distinction between attachment and detachment, you will be in possession of skillful means for avoiding becoming attached to words according to which one proceeds to grasp meanings. Free from the domination of words you will be able to establish yourselves where there will be a 'turning about' in the deepest seat of consciousness by means of which you will attain self-realization of Noble Wisdom. There you will be stamped with the stamp of the powers, self-command, the psychic faculties, and will be endowed with the wisdom and the power of the ten inexhaustible vows, and will become radiant with the variegated rays of the Transformation Bodies. Therewith you will shine without effort like the moon, the sun, the magic wishing-jewel, and at every stage will view things as being of perfect oneness with yourself, uncontaminated by any self-consciousness. It is an inner experience that has no connection with the lower mind-system and its discriminations of words, ideas and philosophical speculations. It shines out with its own clear light.

"After experiencing the 'turning about' in the deepest seat of consciousness, the disciple experiences other Samadhis even to the highest. Before they had attained self-realization of Noble Wisdom they had been influenced by the self-interests of egoism, but after they attain self-realization they will find themselves reacting spontaneously to the impulses of a great and compassionate heart endowed with skillfull and boundless means and sincerely and wholly devoted to the emancipation of all beings.

"Who can trace the invisible path of the man who soars in the sky of liberation, the infinite Void without beginning, whose passions are peace, and over whom pleasures have no power? His path is as difficult to trace as that of the birds in the air. He is calm like the earth that endures; he is steady like a column that is firm; he is pure like a lake that is clear; he is free from Samsara, the ever-returning life-in-death. In the light of his vision he has found his freedom: his thoughts are peace, his words are peace and his work is peace. And when he sees in a clear vision the coming and going of inner events, then he feels the infinite joy of those who see the immortal That, the Nirvana immortal.

"Make an island for yourself. Hasten and strive. Be wise. With the dust of impurities blown off, and free from sinful passions, you will come unto the glorious land of the great. In this land a Buddha called Amitabha right now teaches the Dharma. Why is the Buddha of that region called Amitabha? It is because he is immeasureably bright and glorious, so that his splendor fills the land of the ten regions, and no obstacle can oppose the diffusion of the rays of his glory, for this reason he is called Amitabha."

> The Light of His wisdom is measureless,
> All conditional forms without exception
> Are enveloped in the dawning Light;
> Therefore take refuge in the True Light.

> The clouds of Light have, like space, no
>   hindrances;
> All that have obstructions are not impeded by
>   them;
> There is no one who is not embraced in His Soft
>   Light;
> Take refuge in Him who is beyond thought.

3

BAPTISM BY FIRE

Ἦν τὸ φῶς τὸ ἀληθινόν,
ὃ φωτίζει πάντα ἄνθρωπον
ἐρχόμενον εἰς τὸν κόσμον.

That was the true Light, which lighteth every man that cometh into the world.

———John 1:9

The quotations within this chapter are from the following sources:

The biblical translations used are from the King James Version and the Revised Standard Version.

"The Gospel of Thomas," *The Nag Hammadi Library*, ed. James M. Robinson (New York: HarperCollins, 1988).

◆ ◆ ◆

The tradition of inner light originated in the East and some would have it remain there, believing it foreign to both the letter and the spirit of Christianity. But this assessment can only be made in contradiction to much Biblical scripture. This third tale of light highlights that scripture.

The known historical facts of Jesus' life are quite scanty. The New Testament gospels offer little data. None provide the date of birth or any details of Jesus' life between the ages of 12 to 30. Flavius Josephus, the principle Jewish historian in the first century, mentions Jesus, but only very briefly. It is apparent that during his own lifetime, Jesus remained almost completely unheard of outside the two small provinces of Judea and Galilee.

While Jesus was alive, his teachings remained obscure and little understood, even by his closest disciples. But throughout his life, Jesus hinted at a knowledge and understanding to come. He repeatedly promised his disciples that in time his true identity would be revealed and his teachings would be disseminated throughout the world. Shortly after his death and resurrection, Jesus' promise began to come true. His disciples received the baptism that Jesus had spoken of but never performed while he was alive—the baptism by fire. And Christianity began to spread, like fire, across the Roman Empire.

The following tale gathers those scriptures concerning the real identity of Jesus as "the true light which lighteth every man," as it was revealed in the baptism by fire. The source material is the four New Testament Gospels, the Acts of the Apostles, and the Gospel of Thomas, recently rediscovered in Nag Hammadi, Egypt.

◆ ◆ ◆

It is the fifteenth year of the reign of Tiberius Ceasar (i.e., A.D. 29). There appears in the small Roman province of Judea a strange new Jewish rabbi. He travels along the River Jordan, offering baptism and a message of the coming of the Kingdom of Heaven. Soon he attracts a small band of loyal followers and becomes known as John the Baptist. From all of Judea, including Jerusalem the capital, many travel to the Jordan River to receive his baptism.

John's use of the water baptism is unique. This longstanding custom was traditionally used to initiate Gentile converts into the Jewish faith. But John takes the rite and uses it in a new way. He offers it as a means of purification and repentance for all who wish a rebirth of the spirit. To those he baptizes, John makes a strange proclamation. He says: "I indeed baptize you with water unto repentance: but he that cometh after me is mightier than I, whose shoes I am not worthy to bear: he shall baptize you with the Holy Ghost, and with fire" (Matthew 3:11).

During this time, Jesus is living in Galilee, a province to the north. He hears of John's baptism and decides to travel to the Jordan River and receive it himself. As the rite is performed, the Holy Spirit, "like a dove," descends upon Jesus and John recognizes him as "he who baptizes with the Holy Spirit."

After this event, Jesus undergoes a forty-day period of retreat, fasting, and temptation. He then begins his travels, assembling his own band of close disciples. Each man he calls somehow recognizes him as a great teacher and follows him immediately. He calls Peter, Andrew, James and John, and Matthew. Then Philip is called, who quickly departs to tell his friend Nathanael (aka Bartholomew), that he has found the true teacher prophesied in the scriptures. Nathanael is skeptical but is persuaded to see for himself. As Nathanael approaches, Jesus watches and says, "Behold an Israelite indeed, in whom is no guile!"

Nathanael asks him, "How do you know me?"

Jesus answers, "Before Philip called you, when you were under the fig tree, I saw you."

"Rabbi," Nathanael exclaims, "You are the Son of God! You are the King of Israel!"

But Jesus answers, "Because I said to you, I saw you under the fig tree, do you believe? You shall see greater things than these" (John 1:50).

As soon as the twelve are assembled, Jesus instructs them to preach and to baptize in the manner of John the Baptist. Jesus, however, never performs the water baptism himself. As the group travels through Judea, Jesus' fame quickly grows amid accounts of his miraculous deeds and teachings. There are many healings and other provocative events. The mystery of his identity quickly becomes the object of wide speculation. After a feast in which a large crowd is miraculously fed from scanty provisions of bread and fish, many people follow Jesus across the Sea of Tiberias seeking to know his identity. Jesus' answer is cryptic: "You seek me because you ate your fill of the loaves. Do not labor for the food which perishes, but for the food which endures to eternal life, which the Son of man will give to you. I am the bread of life; he who comes to me shall not hunger, and he who believes in me shall never thirst. For I have come down from heaven, not to do my own will, but the will of him who sent me" (John 6).

These words ignite controversy. Members of the crowd protest, "Is not this Jesus, the son of Joseph, whose father and mother we know? How does he now say, 'I have come down from heaven'?"

Many of Jesus' followers, including his own brothers, now draw back in disbelief. Jesus asks the twelve disciples if they too wish to depart. Peter answers, "Lord, to whom shall we go? You have the words of eternal life."

Jesus and his disciples must now hasten back to Galilee due to death threats from the Judeans. But soon, Jesus' disciples urge him to return to Judea, to the Jerusalem temple to attend the Feast of the Tabernacles. Jesus instructs his disciples to attend the feast in his stead as he remains in Galilee. But at the height of the festival, Jesus appears and begins to preach. The crowds are once again incensed by his words and seek to harm him. On the last day of the feast he again appears, as recorded in the Gospel of John:

"On the last day of the feast, the great day, Jesus stood up and proclaimed, 'If any one thirst, let him come to me and drink. He who believes in me, as the scripture has said, "out of his heart shall flow rivers of living water." ' Now this he said about the Spirit, which those who believed in him were to receive; for as yet the Spirit had not been given, because Jesus was not yet glorified. When they heard these words, some of the people said, 'This is really the prophet.' Others said, 'This is the Christ.' But some said, 'Is the Christ to come from Galilee? Has not the scripture said that the Christ is descended from David, and comes from Bethlehem, the village where David was?' So there was a division among the people over him. Some of them wanted to arrest him, but no one laid hands on him. The officers then went back to the chief priests and Pharisees, who said to them, 'Why did you not bring him?' The officers answered, 'No man ever spoke like this man!' The Pharisees answered them, 'Are you led astry, you also?' " (John 7).

The Pharisees, the Temple masters, now confront Jesus and Jesus speaks to them directly:

"Again Jesus spoke to them, saying, 'I am the light of the world; he who follows me will not walk in darkness, but will have the light of life.' The Pharisees then said to him, 'You are bearing witness to yourself; your testimony is not true.' Jesus answered, 'Even if I do bear witness to myself, my testimony is true, for I know whence I have come and whither I am going, but you do not know whence I come or whither I am going. I bear witness to myself, and the Father who sent me bears witness to me.' They said to him therefore, 'Where is your Father?' Jesus answered, 'You know neither me nor my Father; if you knew me, you would know my Father also.'

"The Jews answered him, 'Are we not right in saying that you are a Samaritan and have a demon?' Jesus answered, 'I have not a demon; but I honor my Father, and you dishonor me. Yet I do not seek my own glory; there is One who seeks it and he will be the judge. Truly, truly, I say to you, if any one keeps my word, he will never see death.' The Jews said to him, 'Now we know that you have a demon. Abraham died, as did the prophets; and you say, If any one keeps my word, he will never taste death. Are you greater than our father Abraham, who died?' Jesus answered, 'Your father Abraham rejoiced that he was to see my day; he saw it and was glad.' The Jews then said to him, 'You are not yet fifty years old, and have you seen Abraham?' Jesus said to them, 'Truly, truly, I say to you, before Abraham was, I am' " (John 8).

The Pharisees and the Judeans are incapable of seeing past Jesus' physical identity. But Jesus is persistent, in this episode at the Temple and throughout his teachings, in presenting himself as an eternal being unlimited by any physical identity. Again and again he presents this identity in metaphorical terms, in the "I am" sayings:

I am the door: by me if any man enter in, he shall be saved (John 10:9).

I am the good shepherd: the good shepherd giveth his life for the sheep (John 10:11).

I am the way, the truth, and the life: no man cometh unto the Father, but by me (John 14:6).

I am the true vine, and my Father is the vine-
dresser (John 15:1).

The disciples, too, are unable to recognize Jesus' true eternal identity. Their full recognition of Jesus will not occur
until the baptism by fire; but now, three of Jesus' followers
receive a foretaste of this recognition in the episode
known as the transfiguration:

"And after six days Jesus took with him Peter and
James and John his brother, and led them up a high mountain apart. And he was transfigured before them, and his
face shone like the sun, and his garments became white as
light. And behold, there appeared to them Moses and
Elijah, talking with him. And Peter said to Jesus, 'Lord, it
is well that we are here; if you wish, I will make three
booths here, one for you and one for Moses and one for
Elijah.' He was still speaking, when lo, a bright cloud over-
shadowed them, and a voice from the cloud said, 'This is
my beloved Son, with whom I am well pleased; listen to
him.' When the disciples heard this, they fell on their
faces, and were filled with awe. But Jesus came and
touched them, saying, 'Rise, and have no fear.' And when
they lifted up their eyes, they saw no one but Jesus only.
And as they were coming down the mountain, Jesus commanded them, 'Tell no one the vision, until the Son of
man is raised from the dead' " (Matthew 17).

Although Jesus instructs Peter, James, and John not to
speak of the vision, Jesus himself often preaches on the
spiritual light. From the Gospel of Thomas, in which
Didymos Thomas records what he calls the "secret sayings" of Jesus, we have these examples:

Jesus said, "It is I who am the light which is above
them all. It is I who am the All. From Me did the
All come forth, and unto Me did the All extend.

Split a piece of wood, and I am there. Life up the stone, and you will find Me there."

His disciples said to Him, "Show us the place where you are, since it is necessary for us to seek it." He said to them, "Whoever has ears, let him hear. There is light within a man of light, and it lights up the whole world. If it does not shine, it is darkness."

Jesus said, "If they say to you, 'Where did you come from?' say to them, 'We came from the light, the place where the light came into being on its own accord and established itself and became manifest through their image . . . "[1]

Matthew, too, quotes Jesus on the light within. In the famous Sermon on the Mount, Jesus tells the gathered crowd: "You are the light of the world. A city set on a hill cannot be hid. Nor do men light a lamp and put it under a bushel, but on a stand, and it gives light to all in the house. Let your light so shine before men, that they may see your good works and give glory to your Father who is in heaven. . . . The eye is the lamp of the body. So if your eye be sound, your whole body will be full of light"(Matthew 5, 6).

Now the time for Jesus' arrest is drawing close. Jesus gathers his disciples and makes a promise of the baptism to come:

"Let not your heart be troubled: ye believe in God, believe also in me. In my Father's house are many mansions: if it were not so, I would have told you. I go to prepare a place for you. And if I go and prepare a place for you, I will come again, and receive you unto myself; that

---

[1]"The Gospel of Thomas," *The Nag Hammadi Library*, ed. James M. Robinson (New York: HarperCollins, 1988, revised edition), pp. 129, 132, 135. Copyright © 1988 E. J. Brill, Leiden, The Netherlands.

where I am, there ye may be also. And whither I go ye know, and the way ye know."

"Thomas saith unto him, 'Lord, we know not whither thou goest; and how can we know the way?'

"Philip saith unto him, 'Lord, shew us the Father, and it sufficeth us.'

"Jesus said unto him, 'Have I been so long with you, and yet hast thou not known me, Philip? He that hath seen me hath seen the Father. If ye love me, keep my commandments. And I will pray the Father, and he shall give you another Comforter, that he may abide with you forever; even the Spirit of truth; whom the world cannot receive, because it seeth him not, neither knoweth him: but ye know him; for he dwelleth with you, and shall be in you. I will not leave you comfortless: I will come to you. Yet a little while, and the world seeth me no more; but ye see me because I live, ye shall live also. At that day ye shall know that I am in my Father, and ye in me, and I in you. He that hath my commandments, and keepeth them, he it is that loveth me: and he that loveth me shall be loved of my Father, and I will love him, and will manifest myself to him. These things have I spoken unto you, being yet present with you. But the Comforter, which is the Holy Ghost, whom the Father will send in my name, he shall teach you all things, and bring all things to your remembrance, whatsoever I have said unto you. Peace I leave with you, my peace I give unto you: not as the world giveth, give I unto you. Let now your heart be troubled, neither let it be afraid. Ye have heard how I said unto you, I go away, and come again unto you. If ye loved me, ye would rejoice, because I said, I go unto the Father: for my Father is greater than I. And now I have told you before it come to pass, that, when it is come to pass, ye might believe. It is expedient for you that I go away: for if I go not away, the Comforter will not come unto you: but if I depart, I will send him unto you' "(John 14, 16).

Jesus then offers this prayer: "Father, glorify thou me in thy own presence with the glory which I had with thee before the world was made. I have manifested thy name to the men whom thou gavest me out of the world; thine they were, and thou gavest them to me, and they have kept thy word. I do not pray that thou shouldst take them out of the world, but that thou shouldst keep them from the evil. I do not pray for these only, but also for those who believe in me through their word, that they may all be one; even as thou, Father, art in me, and I in thee, that they also may be in us, so that the world may believe that thou hast sent me. The glory which thou hast given me I have given to them, that they may be one even as we are one, I in them and thou in me, that they may become perfectly one"(John 17).

Jesus and his disciples now retire to the Garden of Gethsemane where Jesus is arrested. The next day, he stands trial before both the religious and civil authorities and is condemned and crucified the same day. After his death, the disciples gather in hiding, fearing the authorities and the Judean public.

The resurrected Jesus appears to the disciples on 10 occasions. About forty days after his crucifixion, he appears and one final time gives his promise of the baptism to come:

"Wait for the promise of the Father, which ye have heard of me. For John truly baptized with water; but ye shall be baptized with the Holy Ghost not many days hence. It is not for you to know the times or the seasons, which the Father hath put in his own power. But ye shall receive power, after that the Holy Ghost is come upon you: and ye shall be witnesses unto me both in Jerusalem, and in all Judaea, and in Samaria, and unto the uttermost part of the earth" (Acts 1).

The disciples then gather in Jerusalem, and the baptism by fire finally occurs:

"Then returned they unto Jerusalem from the mount called Olivet, which is from Jerusalem a sabbath day's journey. And when they were come in, they went up into an upper room, where abode both Peter, and James, and John, and Andrew, Philip, and Thomas, Bartholomew, and Matthew, James the son of Alphaeus, and Simon Zelotes, and Judas the brother of James. These all continued with one accord in prayer and supplication, with the women, and Mary the mother of Jesus, and with his brethren. And when the day of Pentecost was fully come, they were all with one accord in one place. And suddenly there came a sound from heaven as of a rushing mighty wind, and it filled all the house where they were sitting. And there appeared unto them cloven tongues like as of fire, and it sat upon each of them. And they were all filled with the Holy Ghost, and began to speak with other tongues, as the Spirit gave them utterance" (Acts 1, 2).

The baptism by fire produces a great tranformation in the lives of the disciples. Now without fear, they are empowered to bestow the baptism of the Holy Spirit on others, by the laying on of hands. It is in this manner that Christianity spreads rapidly in the first century. As many as 3000 receive the baptism of the Holy Spirit at one gathering. Initially it is only Jews who receive the baptism of the Holy Spirit, but during a speech by St. Peter at Caesarea, the Holy Spirit descends on Jews and Gentiles alike. Peter is soon rebuked for this incident by the other disciples, but he explains that it was by a will greater than his that the Holy Spirit had descended. The new disciples are called Christians for the first time in Antioch about one year after the crucifixion.

In these earliest Christian times, the baptism by fire is the deciding factor in being a Christian. It is held distinctly separate from the baptism by water, which also continues as a ceremonial initiation into the new church. That there are two separate baptisms is apparent at least twice in the

Acts of the Apostles. On one occasion, Peter and John travel to Samaria after hearing of certain Christians there who had been baptized by water only, but had not yet received the Holy Spirit: "Now when the apostles at Jerusalem heard that Samaria had received the word of God, they sent to them Peter and John who came down and prayed for them that they might receive the Holy Spirit; for it had not yet fallen on any of them, but they had only been baptized in the name of the Lord Jesus. Then they laid their hands on them and they received the Holy Spirit" (Acts 8).

The disciples continue to baptize, heal, and preach. They now, like Christ, promise the gift of light:

> *St. John*: This then is the message which we have heard of him, and declare unto you, that God is light, and in him is no darkness at all.
>
> —1 John 1:5

> But if we walk in the light, as he is in the light, we have fellowship one with another, and the blood of Jesus Christ his Son cleanseth us from all sin.
>
> —1 John 1:7

> *St. Paul*: Awake thou that sleepest, and arise from the dead, and Christ shall give thee light.
>
> —Ephesians 5:14

> *St. Peter*: We have also a more sure word of prophecy; whereunto ye do well that ye take heed, as unto a light that shineth in a dark place, until the day dawn, and the day star arise in your hearts.
>
> —II Peter 1:19

PART II

FIRST-HAND ACCOUNTS

4

THE CONFESSIONS
OF SAINT AUGUSTINE

Intraui in intima mea . . . et uidi qualicumque oculo
animae meae, supra eundem oculum animae meae,
supra mentem meam, lucem inconmutabilem . . . .
Qui nouit ueritatem, nouit eam, et qui nouit eam,
nouit aeternitatem.

I entered into the innermost part of myself . . .
and I saw with the eye of my soul, such as it
was, above the same eye of my soul, above my
mind, the light unchangeable . . . . He who
knows truth knows that light, and he who
knows that light knows eternity.

——St. Augustine
The Confessions

◆ ◆ ◆

In A.D. 400, a highly respected bishop of the Roman Catholic Church was persuaded by his friends to write his memoirs. He agreed to take up the task, but for reasons of his own. He wished to mitigate the high degree of personal adulation he was often accorded by making known his all too human shortcomings. As a result, one of the first, and to this day most candid, spiritual autobiographies was written: *The Confessions of St. Augustine*. The book was widely read in Augustine's own lifetime, and its portrayal of human struggle and ultimate transformation only increased the celebrity and popularity of its author.

Aurelius Augustinus was born in A.D. 354 in the North African coastal city of Hippo. Just a few years before his birth, the terrible persecution of the early Christians had been brought to an end by the Roman Emperor Constantine I, who proclaimed Christianity the official religion of the Roman state. Augustine's mother was a devout Christian and a strong influence, but Augustine resisted the Christian teachings, researching all the many philosophic systems flourishing during that time. He particularly admired the books of Plotinus and personally aspired to the Platonic vision of Beauty. After several years of painful struggle, a profound experience of the inner light overcame him. After this experience, he returned to the Christian scriptures, which had earlier repelled him, and found they now opened to him in perfect clarity. He made the decision to be baptized, sold his property in Milan, and returned to the town of his birth to adopt a monastic way of life. But his plans for a life of prayer and retreat were never realized. Against his wishes, he was nominated for the priesthood. He was ordained Bishop of Hippo and inundated with visitors and official duties the rest of his life. Augustine's autobiography presents one of the very

first written accounts of the inner light experience. The
following tale is taken from five chapters of that book.

♦ ♦ ♦

I pursued my studies of the books of eloquence, a subject
in which I longed to make a name for myself, though my
reason for this was damnable and mere wind, being simply joy in human vanity. In the normal course of study I
came across a book by Cicero, a man whose style, though
not his heart, is almost universally admired. This book of
his contains an exhortation to philosophy; it is called *Hor-
tensius*. Now it was this book which altered my way of
feeling, turned my prayers to you, Lord, yourself, and
gave me different ambitions and desires. Every vain hope
suddenly became worthless to me; my spirit was filled
with an extraordinary and burning desire for the immortality of wisdom, and now I began to rise, so that I might
return to you. I was in my nineteenth year (my father
having died two years previously), and I might be
assumed to be spending the money my mother sent me on
sharpening my tongue; but it was not for the purpose of
sharpening my tongue that I had used this book of
Cicero's; what moved me was not the style, but the
matter.

I was on fire then, my God, I was on fire to leave
earthly things behind and fly back to you, nor did I know
what you would do with me; for with you is wisdom. But
that book inflamed me with the love of wisdom (which is
called "philosophy" in Greek). I was urged on and
inflamed with a passionate zeal to love and seek and
obtain and embrace and hold fast wisdom itself, whatever
it might be.

For about nine years, I was a disciple of the Manichees, and for nearly all of this time I had been waiting
with a kind of boundless longing for the coming of this

man Faustus. For the other Manichees whom I met and who failed to produce any answers to the questions I was raising on these subjects were always putting forward his name and promising me that as soon as Faustus arrived and I was able to discuss matters with him, all these difficulties of mine, together with any more weighty questions that I might care to ask, would be very easily dealt with and very lucidly explained. Well, he did arrive, and I found him a charming man with a very pleasant choice of words; he came out with exactly the same things as the others are always saying, but he did it much more elegantly.

However, my thirst could not be relieved by expensive drinking vessels and a well-dressed waiter. My ears were full already of this stuff, and the arguments themselves did not appear to me to be any better simply because they were better expressed; eloquence did not make them true; nor could I consider the soul wise because the face was attractive and the words well chosen. And as to those who promised me so much of him, they were not good judges of things. Their reason for thinking him wise and intelligent was simply that his way of speaking gave them pleasure.

As a result of this I lost the enthusiasm which I had had for the writings of Manes, and I had all the less confidence in the other Manichaean teachers after I found that the famous Faustus had shown up so badly in many of the questions which perplexed me. However I began to spend much time with him because of his own kind of enthusiasm, which was for literature, and it was literature which I, as professor, was at that time teaching to the young at Carthage.

You acted upon me in such a way that I was persuaded to set out for Rome to teach there the same subjects as I had been teaching in Carthage. I wanted to go to Rome not only because of the higher earnings and the

greater reputation which my friends, who persuaded me
to go, thought I would get there, though these reasons did
have some weight with me at that time; in fact, however,
my main and almost my only reason for going was that I
heard that in Rome the young men followed their studies
in a more orderly manner and were controlled by a stricter
discipline. They were not allowed, for instance, insolently
and at their own pleasure to come rushing into the school
of a man who was not their own teacher; in fact they were
not allowed to enter the school at all without the master's
permission. [Augustine stays in Rome only briefly, accepting a position as professor of rhetoric in Milan.]

I was not yet groaning in prayer for you to help me.
My mind was intent on inquiry and restless in dispute. I
panted for honors, for money, for marriage, I found bitterness and difficulty in following these desires, and your
graciousness to me was shown in the way you would not
allow me to find anything sweet which was not you. Look
into my heart, Lord; for it was you who willed me to
remember all this and to confess it to you. And let my soul
cling to you now that you have freed it from that gripping
birdlime of death! How unhappy it was then! And you
pricked its wound on the quick, so that it might leave
everything else and turn to you, who are above all things
and without whom all things would be nothing—so that it
might turn to you and be cured. I was unhappy indeed,
and you made me really see my unhappiness. It was on a
day when I was preparing a speech to be delivered in
praise of the emperor; there would be a lot of lies in the
speech, and they would be applauded by those who knew
that they were lies. My heart was all wrought up with the
worry of it all and was boiling in a kind of fever of melting
thoughts. I was going along one of the streets of Milan
when I noticed a poor beggar; he was fairly drunk, I suppose, and was laughing and enjoying himself. It was a
sight which depressed me, and I spoke to the friends who

were with me about all the sorrows which come to us because of our own madness. I thought of how I was toiling away, spurred on by my desires and dragging after me the load of my unhappiness and making it all the heavier by dragging it, and it seemed to me that the goal of this and all such endeavors was simply to reach a state of happiness that was free from care; the beggar had reached this state before us, and we, perhaps, might never reach it at all.

No doubt the beggar's joy was not true joy; but it was a great deal truer than the joy which I, with my ambition, was seeking.

All of us who were friends together were depressed by these thoughts. The ones I talked to most about it were Alypius and Nebridius. Alypius was born in the same town as I, and his parents were important people there.

He was my great friend and together with me he was in a state of mental confusion as to what way of life we should take.

There was Nebridius too. He had left his native place near Carthage; he had left Carthage itself, where he usually lived; he had left his rich family estate in the country, left his home, and left his mother, since she was not prepared to follow him. He had come to Milan, and his one reason for doing so was to live with me in a most ardent search for truth and wisdom.

And I, as I looked back over my life, was quite amazed to think of how long a time had passed since my nineteenth year, when I had first become inflamed with a passion for wisdom and had resolved that, when once I found it, I would leave behind me all the empty hopes and deceitful frenzies of vain desires. And now I was in my thirtieth year, still sticking in the same mud, still greedy for the enjoyment of things present, which fled from me and wasted me away, and all the time saying: "I shall find it tomorrow. See, it will become quite clear and I shall grasp it.

"But wait. These worldly things too are sweet; the pleasure they give is not inconsiderable; we must not be too hasty about rejecting them, because it would be a shame to go back to them again. Now think: it would not be very difficult to get some high official appointment, and then what more could I want? I have quite a number of influential friends. Not to press on too fast, I could easily get a governorship. Then I should marry a wife with money, so that she would not increase my expenses. And then I should have nothing more to desire. There have been many great men, well worth imitating, who have devoted themselves to the pursuit of wisdom and have also been married."

The move to get me married went on apace. I made my proposal and the girl was promised to me. In all this my mother played a large part, for, once I was married, she wanted me to be washed in the health-giving water of baptism for which, to her joy, she saw me becoming more fit every day, so that she now felt that her own prayers and your promises were being fulfilled in my faith. Plans for my marriage went ahead and the girl was asked for. She was still about two years below the marriageable age, but I liked her and was prepared to wait.

A group of us, all friends together, after much thought and conversation on how we hated the whole wearisome business of human life, had almost reached the conclusion that we would retire from the crowd and live a life of peace. In order to achieve this we planned to pool our resources and make one common property out of the property of all of us. So, in the sincerity of friendship, there would be no distinction between what belonged to one man or another; all our possessions should count as one piece of property, and the whole should belong to each individual and everything should belong to everybody. It appeared that there might be about ten of us in this society and among these ten were some very rich men—Romanianus in particular, who was a fellow towns-man of ours and had been a great friend of mine from childhood. He had now come to the court at Milan because of some urgent business in connection with his own affairs. He was particularly enthusiastic about the project and his voice had much weight in persuading the rest of us, since his property was much greater than any-body else's. We had decided that two of us should be, like magistrates, appointed every year to deal with the neces-sary provisions for life, while the rest would be left in peace. Next, however, the question was raised as to whether our wives would put up with it—some of us hav-ing wives already and I being anxious to have one. And so the whole scheme, which had been so well worked out, fell to pieces in our hands and was abandoned as imprac-ticable. We went back to our sighing and complaining and our steps continued to follow the broad and well-worn paths of the world.

Meanwhile my sins were being multiplied. The woman with whom I was in the habit of sleeping was torn from my side on the grounds of being an impediment to my marriage, and my heart, which clung to her, was bro-ken and wounded and dropping blood. She had returned to Africa after having made a vow that she would never go to bed with another man, and she had left with me the natural son I had had by her. But I, in my misery, could not follow the example of a woman. I had two years to wait until I could have the girl to whom I was engaged, and I could not bear the delay. So, since I was not so much a lover of marriage as a slave to lust, I found another woman for myself—not, of course, as a wife.

What agonies I suffered, what groans, my God, came from my heart in its labor! And you were listening, though I did not know it. When in silence I strongly urged my question, the quiet contrition of my soul was a great cry to your mercy. You knew what I was suffering, and no man knew it. For how little there was of it which I could put into words even for the hearing of my most intimate friends! How could they hear the tumult of my soul when I had neither time nor language sufficient to express it? Yet all of it reached your hearing, all the roarings and groanings of my heart, and my desire was in front of you and the light of my eyes was not with me. For that light was within and I was out of doors; that was not in space, but my mind was intent on things which were in space, and I could find no place there to rest, and the things of space did not welcome me so that I could say: "It is enough, it is well," nor did they let me go back to where it would have been well enough with me. For I was superior to them, but inferior to you. You are my true joy and I am subject to you, and you have subjected to me the things in your creation which are below me. And this was the correct admixture, the middle way for my salvation—that I should remain in your image and, by serving you, be master of the body.

I was admonished by all this to return to my own self, and, with you to guide me, I entered into the innermost part of myself, and I was able to do this because you were my helper. I entered and I saw with my soul's eye (such as it was) an unchangeable light shining above this eye of my soul and above my mind. It was not the ordinary light which is visible to all flesh, nor something of the same sort, only bigger, as though it might be our ordinary light shining much much more brightly and filling everything with its greatness. No, it was not like that; it was different, entirely different from anything of the kind. Nor was it above my mind as oil floats on water or as the heaven is above the earth. It was higher than I, because it made me, and I was lower because I was made by it. He who knows truth knows that light, and he who knows that light knows eternity. Love knows it. O eternal truth and true love and beloved eternity! You are my God; to you I sigh by day and by night. And when I first knew you, you raised me up so that I could see that there was something to see and that I still lacked the ability to see it. And you beat back the weakness of my sight, blazing upon me with your rays, and I trembled in love and in dread, and I found that I was far distant from you, in a region of total unlikeness, as if I were hearing your voice from on high saying: "I am the food of grown men. Grow and you shall feed upon me. And you will not, as with the food of the body, change me into yourself, but you will be changed into me." And I learned that *Thou, for iniquity, chastenest man and Thou madest my soul to consume away like a spider*. And I said: "Is truth therefore nothing because it is not extended through any kind of space, whether finite or infinite?" And from far away you cried out to me: "I am that I am." And I heard, as one hears things in the heart, and there was no longer any reason at all for me to doubt. I would sooner doubt my own existence than the existence of that truth *which is clearly seen being understood by those things which are made*.

And I felt wonder at the thought that now I loved you and not a phantom instead of you. But I did not stay in the enjoyment of my God; I was swept away to you by your own beauty, and then I was torn away from you by my own weight and fell back groaning toward these lower things. Carnal habit was this weight. But there remained with me the memory of you; I knew with certainty that it was to you that I must cling.

Let me know you, my known; *let me know Thee even as I am known*. Power of my soul, enter into it and fit it for yourself, so that you may have and hold it *without spot or wrinkle*. This is my hope, *therefore do I speak*, and in this hope is my joy, when my joy is healthy. As to the other things of this life, the more we weep for them the less they ought to be wept for, and the less we weep for them the more we ought to weep. For, see, you love the truth, and he that *doth the truth, cometh to the light*. This is what I want to do in my heart, in front of you, in my confession, and in my writing before many witnesses.

Why then do I bother to let men hear my confessions? It is not as though men are likely *to heal all my infirmities*. Men are a race very inquisitive about other people's lives, very lazy in improving their own. Why should they want to hear from me what I am, when they do not want to hear from you what they are?

So in confessing not only what I have been but what I am the advantage is this: I make my confession not only in front of you, in a secret *exultation with trembling*, with a secret sorrow and with hope, but also in the ears of the believing sons of men, companions in my joy and sharers in my mortality, my fellow citizens and fellow pilgrims— those who have gone before and those who follow after and those who are on the road with me.

There is no doubt in my mind, Lord, that I love you. I feel it with certainty. You struck my heart with your word, and I loved you. But, see, *heaven and earth and all that therein is* on every side are telling me to love you, and they never stop saying it to all men, *that they may be without excuse*. But more deeply *wilt Thou have mercy on whom Thou wilt have mercy, and wilt have compassion on whom Thou hast had compassion*; otherwise heaven and earth are telling your praises to deaf ears.

But what do I love when I love you? Not the beauty of the body nor the glory of time, not the brightness of light shining so friendly to the eye, not the sweet and various melodies of singing, not the fragrance of flowers and unguents and spices, not manna and honey, not limbs welcome to the embraces of the flesh: it is not these that I love when I love my God. And yet I do love a kind of light, melody, fragrance, food, embracement when I love my

God; for He is the light, the melody, the fragrance, the food, the embracement of my inner self—there where is a brilliance that space cannot contain, a sound that time cannot carry away, a perfume that no breeze disperses, a taste undiminished by eating, a clinging together that no satiety will sunder. This is what I love when I love my God.

Late it was that I loved you, beauty so ancient and so new, late I loved you! And, look, you were within me and I was outside, and there I sought for you and in my ugliness I plunged into the beauties that you have made. You were with me, and I was not with you. Those outer beauties kept me far from you, yet if they had not been in you, they would not have existed at all. You called, you cried out, you shattered my deafness: you flashed, you shone, you scattered my blindness: you breathed perfume, and I drew in my breath and I pant for you: I tasted, and I am hungry and thirsty: you touched me, and I burned for your peace.

5

THE SUTRA OF HUI-NENG

Within the domain
of our mind
There is a Buddha
of Enlightenment
Who sends forth
a powerful light.

————Hui-Neng,
The Sutra of Hui-Neng

The excerpts in this chapter, including the long quotation in the introduction, are taken from the following source:

The Sutra of Hui-Neng, translated by Wong Mou-Lam. Published in *The Diamond Sutra and The Sutra of Hui Neng*, translated by A.F. Price and Wong Mou-Lam (Boston: Shambhala, 1969), from chapters 1–4, 8, 10. Reprinted by arrangement with Shambhala Publications, Inc., Boston, MA, and The Buddhist Society, London.

◆ ◆ ◆

Six hundred years after the passing of the Buddha (about A.D. 67), Buddhism spread from Gautama's native India into China. There, with the interplay of Taoism, it emerged as the great Chinese religion now known as Zen. (In China, Zen is called *Ch'an*, but we take the liberty of using its more widely known Japanese name.)

The man most responsible for bringing Zen into the world was Hui-Neng (638–713), a common laborer who became the Sixth Zen Patriarch. The events by which Hui-Neng inherited the special robe and begging bowl of the Patriarchate are recorded in the *Sutra of Hui-Neng*. This sutra was first translated into English in 1930; thus the West's exposure to Zen is very recent.

Among Buddhist scripture, the designation *Sutra* is reserved for sermons spoken by Lord Buddha or by great Bodhisattvas. The *Sutra of Hui-Neng* is the only sermon by a native of China to receive this honor. Reading a Sutra is considered a blessing in itself, capable of transporting the reader to higher understanding. In the foreword to an early American edition of the Sutra is this advice:

"The Sutra extends to you, the reader, the possibility of coming to the full realization of Enlightenment; in, of, and through your own understanding. You need not turn to any ritual, dogma, or creed; just keep reading it. The only worthwhile practice is to understand. When you have reached understanding, you will realize the Light never seen on land or sea. You will not have to do, or strain for gain; you will know Who you Are; then you will only have to Be. Learn to feel-think from the depths of Being. Discard sentimentality; feel the real. Know that all which our senses contact is but a limited expression of unity in diversity. Know that beyond objectivity and subjectivity is That which you Are. When you can experience this, you realize the Essence. Then intuitive spontaneity is functional for you. If you can let this Sutra happen for you, you will enjoy 'unendurable pleasure indefinitely prolonged.' FALL AWAKE, my friend! May all beings be well, May all beings be happy."

♦ ♦ ♦

PART ONE

The Robe of the Patriarch

Once, when the Patriarch had arrived at Pao Lin Monastery, Prefect Wei and other officials went there to ask him to deliver public lectures on Buddhism in the hall of Ta Fan Temple. In due course, there were assembled in the lecture hall Prefect Wei, government officials, Confucian scholars, Zen monks and nuns, Taoists and laymen to the number of about one thousand. After the Patriarch had taken his seat, the congregation in a body paid him homage and asked him to preach on the fundamental laws of Buddhism. Whereupon, His Holiness delivered the following address:

Learned Audience, our Essence of Mind, which is the seed or kernel of enlightenment, is pure by nature, and by making use of this mind alone we can reach Buddhahood directly. Now let me tell you something about my own life and how I came into possession of the esoteric teaching of the Zen School.

My father, a native of Fan Yang, was dismissed from his official post and banished to be a commoner in Hsin Chou in Kwangtung. I was unlucky in that my father died when I was very young, leaving my mother poor and miserable. We moved to Kwang Chou and were then in very bad circumstances.

I was selling firewood in the market one day, when one of my customers ordered some to be brought to his shop. Upon delivery being made and payment received, I left the shop, outside of which I found a man reciting a sutra. As soon as I heard the text of this sutra my mind at once became enlightened. Thereupon I asked the man the name of the book he was reciting and was told that it was the Diamond Sutra. I further enquired whence he came and why he recited this particular sutra. He replied that he came from Tung Ch'an Monastery in the Huang Mei District of Ch'i Chou; that the Abbot in charge of this temple was Hung Yen, the Fifth Patriarch; that there were about one thousand disciples under him.

It must be due to my good karma in past lives that I heard about this, and that I was given ten taels for the maintenance of my mother by a man who advised me to go to Huang Mei to interview the Fifth Patriarch. After arrangements had been made for her, I left for Huang Mei, which took me less than thirty days to reach.

I then went to pay homage to the Patriarch, and was asked where I came from and what I expected to get from him. I replied, "I am a commoner from Hsin Chou of Kwangtung. I have travelled far to pay you respect and I ask for nothing but Buddhahood."

"You are a native of Kwangtung, a barbarian? How can you expect to be a Buddha?" asked the Patriarch.

I replied, "Although there are northern men and southern men, north and south make no difference to their Buddha-nature. A barbarian is different from your Holiness physically, but there is no difference in our Buddha-nature." He was going to speak further to me, but the presence of other disciples made him stop short. He then ordered me to join the crowd to work.

"May I tell Your Holiness," said I, "that Prajna (transcendental wisdom) often rises in my mind. When one does not go astray from one's own Essence of Mind, one may be called the 'field of merits.' I do not know what work Your Holiness would ask me to do."

"This barbarian is too bright," he remarked, "Go to the stable and speak no more." I then withdrew myself to the backyard and was told by a lay brother to split firewood and to pound rice.

More than eight months after, the Patriarch saw me one day and said, "I know your knowledge of Buddhism is very sound, but I have to refrain from speaking to you lest evildoers should do you harm. Do you understand?"

"Yes, Sir, I do," I replied. "To avoid people taking notice of me, I dare not go near your hall."

The Patriarch one day assembled all his disciples and said to them, "Go and seek Prajna (wisdom) in your own mind and then write me a stanza about it. He who understands what the Essence of Mind is will be given the robe (the insignia of the Patriarchate) and the Dharma (i.e., the esoteric teaching of the Zen school), and I shall make him the Sixth Patriarch. Go away quickly. Delay not in writing the stanza, as deliberation is quite unnecessary and of no use. The man who has realised the Essence of Mind can speak of it at once, as soon as he is spoken to about it; and he cannot lose sight of it, even when engaged in battle."

Having received this instruction, the disciples withdrew and said to one another, "It is of no use for us to concentrate our mind to write the stanza and submit it to His Holiness, since the Patriarchate is bound to be won by Shen Hsiu, our instructor. And if we write perfunctorily, it will only be a waste of energy." Upon hearing this, all of them made up their minds not to write.

Meanwhile, Shen Hsiu reasoned thus with himself. "Considering that I am their teacher, none of them will take part in the competition. I wonder whether I should write a stanza and submit it to His Holiness. If I do not, how can the Patriarch know how deep or superficial my knowledge is? If my object is to get the Dharma, my motive is a pure one. If I were after the Patriarchate, then it would be bad. In that case, my mind would be that of a worldling and my action would amount to robbing the Patriarch's holy seat. But if I do not submit the stanza, I shall never have a chance of getting the Dharma. A very difficult point to decide, indeed!"

When Shen Hsiu had composed his stanza he made several attempts to submit it to the Patriarch, but as soon as he went near the hall his mind was so perturbed that he sweated all over. He could not screw up courage to submit it, although in the course of four days he made altogether thirteen attempts to do so.

Then he suggested to himself, "It would be better for me to write it on the wall of the corridor and let the Patriarch see it for himself. If he approves it, I shall come out to pay homage, and tell him that it is done by me; but if he disapproves it, then I shall have wasted several years in this mountain in receiving homage from others which I by no means deserve! In that case, what progress have I made in learning Buddhism?"

At 12 o'clock that night he went secretly with a lamp to write the stanza on the wall of the south corridor, so that the Patriarch might know what spiritual insight he had attained. The stanza read:

> Our body is the Bodhi-tree
> And our mind a mirror bright.
> Carefully we wipe them hour by hour,
> And let no dust alight.

Two days after, it happened that a young boy who was passing by the room where I was pounding rice recited loudly the stanza written by Shen Hsiu. As soon as I heard it, I knew at once that the composer of it had not yet realised the Essence of Mind. I told the boy that I wished to recite the stanza too, so that I might have an affinity with its teaching in future life. I also told him that although I had been pounding rice there for eight months I had never been to the hall, and that he would have to show me where the stanza was to enable me to make obeisance to it.

The boy took me there and I asked him to read it to me, as I am illiterate. A petty officer of the Chiang Chou District named Chang Yih-Yung, who happened to be there, read it out to me. When he had finished reading I told him that I also had composed a stanza, and asked him to write it for me. "Extraordinary indeed," he exclaimed, "that you also can compose a stanza!"

"Don't despise a beginner," said I, "if you are a seeker of supreme enlightenment."

"Dictate your stanza," said he. "I will take it down for you. But do not forget to deliver me, should you succeed in getting the Dharma!"

My stanza read:

> There is no Bodhi-tree
> Nor stand of mirror bright.
> Since all is void,
> Where can the dust alight?

Next day the Patriarch came secretly to the room where the rice was pounded. Seeing that I was working there with a stone pestle, he said to me, "A seeker of the Path risks his life for the Dharma. Should he not do so?" Then he asked, "Is the rice ready?"

"Ready long ago," I replied, "only waiting for the sieve." He knocked the mortar thrice with his stick and left.

Knowing what his message meant, in the third watch of the night I went to his room. Using the robe as a screen so that none could see us, he expounded the Diamond Sutra to me. When he came to the sentence, "One should use one's mind in such a way that it will be free from any attachment," I at once became thoroughly enlightened, and realised that all things in the universe are the Essence of Mind itself.

"Who would have thought," I said to the Patriarch, "that the Essence of Mind is intrinsically pure! Who would have thought the Essence of Mind is intrinsically free from becoming or annihilation! Who would have thought that the Essence of Mind is intrinsically self-sufficient! Who would have thought that the Essence of Mind is intrinsically free from change! Who would have thought that all things are the manifestation of the Essence of Mind!"

Knowing that I had realised the Essence of Mind, the Patriarch said, "For him who does not know his own mind there is no use learning Buddhism. On the other hand, if he knows his own mind and sees intuitively his own nature, he is a Hero, a 'Teacher of gods and men,' 'Buddha.' "

Thus, to the knowledge of no one, the Dharma was transmitted to me at midnight, and consequently I became the inheritor of the teaching of the "Sudden School" as well as of the robe and the begging bowl.

"You are now the Sixth Patriarch," said he. "Take good care of yourself, and deliver as many sentient beings as possible. Spread and preserve the teaching, and don't let it come to an end.

He further said, "When the Patriarch Bodhidharma first came to China, most Chinese had no confidence in him, and so this robe was handed down as a testimony from one Patriarch to another. As to the Dharma, this is transmitted from heart to heart, and the recipient must realise it by his own efforts. From time immemorial it has been the practice for one Buddha to pass to his successor the quintessence of the Dharma, and for one Patriarch to transmit to another the esoteric teaching from heart to heart. As the robe may give cause for dispute, you are the last one to inherit it. Should you hand it down to your successor, your life would be in imminent danger. Now leave this place as quickly as you can, lest someone should do you harm."

"Whither should I go?" I asked.

"At Huai you stop and at Hui you seclude yourself," he replied.

Part Two

Mind in Motion

Sometime after, I reached Ts'ao Ch'i and I had to take refuge in Szu Hui, where I stayed with a party of hunters for a period as long as fifteen years.

One day I bethought myself that I ought not to pass a secluded life all the time, and that it was high time for me to propagate the Law. Accordingly I left there and went to the Fa Hsin Temple in Canton.

At that time Monk Yin Tsung, Master of the Dharma, was lecturing on the Maha Parinirvana Sutra in the Temple. It happened that one day, when a pennant was blown about by the wind, two monks entered into a dispute as to what it was that was in motion, the wind or the pennant. As they could not settle their difference I submitted to them that it was neither, and that what actually moved was their own mind. The whole assembly was startled by what I said, and Monk Yin Tsung invited me to take a seat of honour and questioned me about various knotty points in the Sutras.

Seeing that my answers were precise and accurate, and that they showed something more than book-knowledge, he said to me, "Lay Brother, you must be an extraordinary man. I was told long ago that the inheritor of the Fifth Patriarch's robe and Dharma had come to the South. Very likely you are the man."

To this I politely assented. He immediately made obeisance and asked me to show the assembly the robe and the begging bowl which I had inherited.

He further asked what instruction I had when the Fifth Patriarch transmitted me the Dharma.

"Apart from a discussion on the realisation of the Essence of Mind," I replied, "he gave me no other instruction. The Wisdom of Enlightenment is inherent in every one of us. It is because of the delusion under which our mind works that we fail to realise it ourselves, and that we have to seek the advice and the guidance of enlightened ones before we can know our own Essence of Mind. You should know that so far as Buddha-nature is concerned, there is no difference between an enlightened man and an ignorant one. What makes the difference is that one realises it, while the other is ignorant of it. Intrinsically our transcendental nature is void and not a single thing can be attained. It is the same with the Essence of Mind, which is a state of 'Absolute Void.' When you hear me talk about the Void, do not at once fall into the idea of vacuity (because this involves the heresy of the doctrine of annihilation). It is of the utmost importance that we should not fall into this idea. The illimitable Void of the universe is capable of holding myriads of things of various shape and form, such as the sun, the moon, stars, mountains, rivers, worlds, springs, rivulets, bushes, woods, good men, bad men. Space takes in all these, and so does the voidness of our nature. We say that the Essence of Mind is great because it embraces all things, since all things are within our nature. What the ignorant merely talk about, wise men put into actual practice with their mind. You should know that the mind is very great in capacity, since it pervades the whole universe. When we use it, we can know something of everything, and when we use it to full capacity we shall know all. All in one and one in all.

When the Fifth Patriarch preached to me I became enlightened immediately after he had spoken, and spontaneously realised the real nature of Tathata. For this reason it is my particular object to propagate the teaching of this "Sudden School," so that learners may find Bodhi at once and realise their true nature by introspection of mind. Should they fail to enlighten themselves, they should ask the pious and learned Buddhists who understand the teaching of the Highest School to show them the right way. The distinction between the "Sudden" and the "Gradual" School does not really exist; the only difference is that by nature some men are quick-witted, while others are dull in understanding. Those who are enlightened realise the truth in a sudden, while those who are under delusion have to train themselves gradually. But such a difference will disappear when we know our own mind and realise our own nature. Therefore these terms, gradual and sudden, are more apparent than real.

To keep our mind free from defilement under all circumstances is called "Idea-lessness." Our mind should stand aloof from circumstances, and on no account should we allow them to influence the function of our mind. But it is a great mistake to suppress our mind from all thinking. Mark this, treaders of the Path. When we use Prajna for introspection we are illumined within and without, and in a position to know our own mind. To know our mind is to obtain liberation. To obtain liberation is to attain Samadhi of Prajna, which is "thoughtlessness." What is "thoughtlessness"? "Thoughtlessness" is to see and to know all things with a mind free from attachment. When in use it pervades everywhere, and yet it sticks nowhere. What we have to do is to purify our mind. Those who understand the way of "thoughtlessness" will know everything, will have the experience all Buddhas have had, and attain Buddhahood.

PART THREE

The Pure Land of the West

One day Prefect Wei entertained the Patriarch and asked him to preach to a big gathering. At the end of the feast, Prefect Wei asked him to mount the pulpit (to which the Patriarch consented). After bowing twice reverently, in company with other officials, scholars, and commoners, Prefect Wei said, "I have heard what Your Holiness preached. It is really so deep that it is beyond our mind and speech, and I have certain doubts which I hope you will clear up for me."

"If you have any doubts," replied the Patriarch, "please ask, and I will explain."

Prefect Wei then asked: "I notice that it is a common practice for monks and laymen to recite the name of Amitabha with the hope of being born in the Pure Land of the West. To clear up my doubts, will you please tell me whether it is possible for them to be born there or not."

"Listen to me carefully, Sir," replied the Patriarch, "and I will explain. According to the Sutra spoken by the Bhagavat in Shravasti City for leading people to the Pure Land of the West, it is quite clear that the Pure Land is not far from here, for the distance in mileage is 108,000, which really represents the "ten evils" and "eight errors" within us. To those of inferior mentality certainly it is far away, but to superior men we may say that it is quite near. While ignorant men recite the name of Amitabha and pray to be born in the Pure Land, the enlightened purify their mind, for, as the Buddha said, 'When the mind is pure, the Buddha land is simultaneously pure.'

"Now, I advise you, Learned Audience, first to do away with the 'ten evils'; then we shall have travelled one hundred thousand miles. For the next step, do away with the 'eight errors,' and this will mean another eight thousand miles traversed. If we can realise the Essence of Mind at all times and behave in a straightforward manner on all occasions, in the twinkling of an eye we may reach the Pure Land.

"Sirs, this physical body of ours is a city. Our eyes, ears, nose, and tongue are the gates. There are five external gates, while the internal one is ideation. The mind is the ground. The Essence of Mind is the King who lives in the domain of the mind. While the Essence of Mind is in, the King is in, and our body and mind exist. When the Essence of Mind is out, there is no King and our body and mind decay. We should work for Buddhahood within the Essence of Mind, and we should not look for it apart from ourselves. He who is kept in ignorance of his Essence of Mind is an ordinary being. He who is enlightened in his Essence of Mind is a Buddha. Within the domain of our mind, there is a Tathagata [Buddha] of enlightenment who sends forth a powerful light which illumines externally the six gates (of sensation) and purifies them. This light is strong enough to pierce through the six Kama Heavens; and when it is turned inwardly it eliminates at once the three poisonous elements, purges away our sins which might lead us to the hells or other evil realms, and enlightens us thoroughly within and without, so that we are not different from those born in the pure Land of the West."

PART FOUR

Parting Instructions

In the 7th Moon of the year of Jên Tzú, the 1st year of T'ai Chi or Yen Ho Era, the Pariarch sent some of his disciples to Hsin Chou to have a shrine built within the Kuo En monastery, with instructions that the work should be completed as soon as possible. Next year, when summer was well-nigh spent, the shrine was duly completed.

On the 1st day of the 7th Moon, the Patriarch assembled his disciples and addressed them as follows:

"I am going to leave this world by the 8th Moon. Should you have any doubts on the doctrine please ask me in time, so that I can clear them up for you."

Seeing that the Patriarch would pass away in the near future, the head Monk, Fa Hai, after prostrating himself twice asked, "Sir, upon your entering into Nirvana, who will be the inheritor of the robe of the Dharma?"

"All my sermons," replied the Patriarch, "from the time I preached in Ta Fan monastery, may be copied out for circulation in a volume to be entitled *Sutra Spoken on the High Seat of the Treasure of the Law.* Take good care of it and hand it down from one generation to another for the salvation of all sentient beings. He who preaches in accordance with its teachings preaches the Orthodox Dharma. As to the transmission of the robe, this practice is to be discontinued. Why? Because you all have implicit faith in my teaching, and being free from all doubts you are able to carry out the lofty object of our School."

On the 8th day of the 7th Moon, the Patriarch gave a sudden order to his disciples to get ready a boat for Hsin Chou (his native place). In a body they entreated him earnestly and pitifully to stay.

"After your visit to Hsin Chou," entreated the assembly, "please return here sooner or later."

"Fallen leaves go back to where the root is," replied the Patriarch.

Then they asked, "To whom, Sir, do you transmit the Womb of the Dharma Eye?"

"Men of principle will get it, and those who are mindless will understand it."

On the 3rd day of the 8th Moon of the year of Kuei Chou, the 2nd Year of Hsin T'ien Era (A.D. 713), after taking food at the Kuo En Monastery, the Patriarch addressed his disciples as follows:

"Please sit down, for I am going to say good-bye." Thereupon Fa Hai spoke to the Patriarch, "Sir, will you please leave to posterity definite instructions whereby people under delusion may realise the Buddha nature."

Replied the Patriarch: "Within our mind there is a Buddha, and that Buddha within is the real Buddha. If Buddha is not to be sought within our mind, where shall we find the real Buddha? Doubt not that Buddha is within your mind, apart from which nothing can exist.

"Take good care of yourselves. After my passing away, do not follow the worldly tradition, and cry or lament. Neither should messages of condolence be accepted, nor mourning be worn. What you should do is to know your own mind and realise your own Buddha-nature, which neither rests nor moves, neither becomes nor ceases to be."

He sat reverently until the third watch of the night. Then he said abruptly to his disciples, "I am going now," and in a sudden passed away. A peculiar fragrance pervaded his room, and a lunar rainbow appeared which seemed to join up earth and sky. The trees in the wood turned white, and birds and beasts cried mournfully.

6

THE MECCAN PILGRIMAGE
OF AL-GHAZALI

خَلَوْا مِن قَبْلِكُمْ وَمَوْعِظَةً لِلْمُتَّقِينَ

Allah is the Light
of the heavens
and the earth.

————The Koran
Surah 24:35

The excerpts within this chapter are from the
following sources:

The Confessions of Al Ghazali, The Wisdom of the
East Series, edited by L. Cranmer-Byng and Dr.
S.A. Kapadia (New York, Dutton, 1909), from
Parts 1, 3, 6, 7, 8.

Readings from the Mystics of Islam, translated by
Margaret Smith (London: Luzac and Co., Ltd.,
1972) pp. 27, 115, 116, 89, 90.

◆ ◆ ◆

The laws of orthodox Islam are found in the Holy Koran. To be a Moslem requires obedience to the precepts enumerated in this book. A Moslem must make a profession of faith, follow rituals of daily worship, undergo periodic fasting, and make a pilgrimage to Mecca at least once in his life. But from the earliest days of Islam, there were those who were not satisfied by a mere testimony of faith and obedience to ritual. These men and women retired from society to seek direct, personal experience of God. They became known as Sufis, so named for their garments of white wool (*suf*).

It is due to the lives and experiences of the Sufis that the inner light tradition is found in Islam. The first Sufis encountered much opposition from orthodox Islam due to their lifestyle of retreat, monasticism and asceticism, which are all emphatically denounced in the Koran. But the Sufis continued to base their way of life on an esoteric reading of the Koranic texts, stressing those verses which suggest the nearness of God, such as "He hears all and is near at hand" (Verse 34:50), and "We created man. We know the promptings of his soul, and are closer to him than the vein of his neck" (Verse 50:16).

It was not until the life of Al-Ghazali (1058–1111) that Sufism found some degree of acceptance in the orthodox Islamic world. Because of the highly revered philosophical writings of Al-Ghazali (in particular his *Revivification of the Sciences of Religion*), Sufism became an optional subject of study in certain mosques.

Al-Ghazali was born in Tus, in northeast Persia, now Iran. He excelled in his youthful studies to the point of gaining the attention of the powerful vizier, Nizam-al-Mulk, a ruler dedicated to learning. Al-Ghazali was sent to Baghdad, which was at that time a great cultural city possessing no fewer than thirty-six libraries. He was

appointed chief professor at Nizamiyah College in Baghdad and soon attracted up to three hundred students at
his lectures. In addition to teaching, Al-Ghazali was called
upon to make judicial decisions according to Islamic law.
His wealth and position increased such that the greatness
of his household rivaled that of the vizier's himself.

At the height of his reputation, however, he suffered
an emotional and physical collapse. Upon recovering, he
announced his resignation and his intent to make the pilgrimage to Mecca. Most of the remainder of his life was
spent as a wandering Sufi, in such places as Damascus
and Jerusalem. He was finally persuaded by the government to resume his lecturing. He taught and wrote several
books and died in Tus, the small village of his birth.

Toward the end of his life, apparently at the request of
his students, Al-Ghazali wrote an autobiographical
account of his scholarly life and his conversion to Sufism.
He therein explains his real reasons for giving up his brilliant career and gives an account of some of his experiences following the Sufi path. He entitled his autobiography *Deliverance from Error*.

♦   ♦   ♦

You have asked me, O brother in the faith, to expound the
aim and the mysteries of religious sciences, the bounda-
ries and depths of theological doctrines. You wish to know
my experiences while disentangling truth lost in the med-
ley of sects and divergencies of thought, and how I have
dared to climb from the low levels of traditional belief to
the topmost summit of assurance. You desire to learn
what I have borrowed, first of all from scholastic theology;
and secondly from the method of the Ta'limites, who, in
seeking truth, rest upon the authority of a leader; and
why, thirdly, I have been led to reject philosophic systems; and finally, what I have accepted of the doctrine of

the Sufis, and the sum total of truth which I have gathered in studying every variety of opinion. You ask me why, after resigning at Bagdad a teaching post which attracted a number of hearers, I have, long afterwards, accepted a similar one at Nishapur. Convinced as I am of the sincerity which prompts your inquiries, I proceed to answer them, invoking the help and protection of God.

Know then, my brothers (may God direct you in the right way), that the diversity in beliefs and religions, and the variety of doctrines and sects which divide men, are like a deep ocean strewn with shipwrecks, from which very few escape safe and sound.

From the period of adolescence, that is to say, previous to reaching my twentieth year to the present time when I have passed my fiftieth, I have ventured into this vast ocean; I have fearlessly sounded its depths, and, like a resolute diver, I have penetrated its darkness and dared its dangers and abysses. I have interrogated the beliefs of each sect and scrutinised the mysteries of each doctrine, in order to disentangle truth from error and orthodoxy from heresy.

Having noticed how easily the children of Christians become Christians, and the children of Moslems embrace Islam, I was moved by a keen desire to learn what was this innate disposition in the child, the nature of the accidental beliefs imposed on him by the authority of his parents and his masters, and finally the unreasoned convictions which he derives from their instructions.

Struck with the contradictions which I encountered in endeavouring to disentangle the truth and falsehood of these opinions, I was led to make the following reflection: "The search after truth being the aim which I propose to myself, I ought in the first place to ascertain what are the bases of certitude." In the next place I recognised that certitude is the clear and complete knowledge of things, such knowledge as leaves no room for doubt nor possibility of error and conjecture, so that there remains no room in the mind for error to find an entrance.

I then examined what knowledge I possessed, and discovered that in none of it, with the exception of sense-perceptions and necessary principles, did I enjoy that degree of certitude which I have just described. I then sadly reflected as follows: "We cannot hope to find truth except in matters which carry their evidence in themselves—that is to say, in sense-perceptions and necessary principles; we must therefore establish these on a firm basis. Is my absolute confidence in sense-perceptions and on the infallibility of necessary principles analogous to the confidence which I formerly possessed in matters believed on the authority of others?

To this argument I remained some time without reply; a reflection drawn from the phenomena of sleep deepened my doubt. "Do you not see," I reflected, "that while asleep you assume your dreams to be indisputably real? Once awake, you recognise them for what they are—baseless chimeras. Who can assure you, then, of the reliability of notions which, when awake, you derive from the senses and from reason? In relation to your present state they may be real; but it is possible also that you may enter upon another state of being which will bear the same relation to your present state as this does to your condition when asleep. In that new sphere you will recognise that the conclusions of reason are only chimeras."

This possible condition is, perhaps, that which the Sufis call "ecstasy" ("hāl"), that is to say, according to them, a state in which, absorbed in themselves and in the suspension of sense-perceptions; they have visions beyond the reach of intellect. Perhaps also Death is that state, according to that saying of the Prince of prophets: "Men are asleep; when they die, they wake." Our present life in relation to the future is perhaps only a dream, and man, once dead, will see things in direct opposition to those now before his eyes; he will then understand that word of the Koran, "To-day we have removed the veil from thine eyes and thy sight is keen."

Such thoughts as these threatened to shake my reason, and I sought to find an escape from them. But how? In order to disentangle the knot of this difficulty, a proof was necessary. Now a proof must be based on primary assumptions, and it was precisely these of which I was in doubt. This unhappy state lasted about two months, during which I was, not, it is true, explicitly or by profession, but morally and essentially, a thorough-going sceptic.

God at last deigned to heal me of this mental malady; my mind recovered sanity and equilibrium, the primary assumptions of reason recovered with me all their stringency and force. I owed my deliverance, not to a concatenation of proofs and arguments, but to the light which God caused to penetrate into my heart—the light which illuminates the threshold of all knowledge. To suppose that certitude can be only based upon formal arguments is to limit the boundless mercy of God. Some one asked the Prophet the explanation of this passage in the Divine Book: "God opens to Islam the heart of him whom He chooses to direct." "That is spoken," replied the Prophet, "of the light which God sheds in the heart." "And how can man recognise that light?" he was asked. "By his detachment from this world of illusion and by a secret drawing towards the eternal world," the Prophet replied.

On another occasion he said: "God has created His creatures in darkness, and then has shed upon them His light." It is by the help of this light that the search for truth must be carried on. As by His mercy this light descends from time to time among men, we must ceaselessly be on the watch for it. This is also corroborated by another saying of the Apostle: "God sends upon you, at certain times, breathings of His grace; be prepared for them."

My object in this account is to make others understand with what earnestness we should search for truth, since it leads to results we never dreamt of.

When God in the abundance of His mercy had healed me of this malady, I ascertained that those who are engaged in the search for truth may be divided into three groups.

I. Scholastic theologians, who profess to follow theory and speculation.

II. The Philosophers, who profess to rely upon formal logic.

III. The Sufis, who call themselves the elect of God and possessors of intuition and knowledge of the truth by means of ecstasy.

"The truth," I said to myself, "must be found among these three classes of men who devote themselves to the search for it. If it escapes them, one must give up all hope of attaining it. Having once surrendered blind belief, it is impossible to return to it, for the essence of such belief is to be unconscious of itself. As soon as this unconsciousness ceases it is shattered like a glass whose fragments cannot be again reunited except by being cast again into the furnace and refashioned." Determined to follow these paths and to search out these systems to the bottom, I proceeded with my investigations in the following order: Scholastic theology; philosophical systems; and, finally Sufism.

Commencing with theological science, I carefully studied and meditated upon it. I read the writings of the authorities in this department and myself composed several treatises. I recognised that this science, while sufficing its own requirements, could not assist me in arriving at the desired goal. In short, its object is to preserve the purity of orthodox beliefs from all heretical innovation. God, by means of His Apostle, has revealed to His creatures a belief which is true as regards their temporal and eternal interests; the chief articles of it are laid down in the Koran and in the traditions.

I proceeded from the study of scholastic theology to that of philosophy. It was plain to me that, in order to discover where the professors of any branch of knowledge have erred, one must make a profound study of that science; must equal, nay surpass, those who know most of it, so as to penetrate into secrets of it unknown to them. Only by this method can they be completely answered, and of this method I can find no trace in the theologians of Islam. In theological writings devoted to the refutation of philosophy I have only found a tangled mass of phrases full of contradictions and mistakes, and incapable of deceiving, I will not say a critical mind, but even the common crowd. Convinced that to dream of refuting a doctrine before having thoroughly comprehended it was like shooting at an object in the dark, I devoted myself zealously to the study of philosophy; but in books only and without the aid of a teacher. I gave up to this work all the leisure remaining from teaching and from composing works on law. There were then attending my lectures three hundred of the students of Bagdad. With the help of God, these studies, carried on in secret, so to speak, put me in a condition to thoroughly comprehend philosophical systems within a space of two years. I then spent about a year in meditating on these systems after having thoroughly understood them. I turned them over and over in my mind till they were thoroughly clear of all obscurity. In this manner I acquired a complete knowledge of all their subterfuges and subtleties, of what was truth and what was illusion in them.

The philosophical systems, in spite of their number and variety, may be reduced to three (1) The Materialists; (2) The Naturalists; (3) The Theists.

(1) *The Materialists*. They reject an intelligent and omnipotent Creator and Disposer of the Universe. In their view the world exists from all eternity and had no author. The animal comes from semen and semen from the animal; so it has always been and will always be; those who maintain this doctrine are atheists.

(2) *The Naturalists*. These devote themselves to the study of nature and of the marvellous phenomena of the animal and vegetable world. Having carefully analysed animal organs with the help of anatomy, struck with the wonders of God's work and with the wisdom therein revealed, they are forced to admit the existence of a wise Creator Who knows the end and purpose of everything. And certainly no one can study anatomy and the wonderful mechanism of living things without being obliged to confess the profound wisdom of Him Who has framed the bodies of animals and especially of man. But carried away by their natural researches they believed that the existence of a being absolutely depended upon the proper equilibrium of its organism. According to them, as the latter perishes and is destroyed, so is the thinking faculty which is bound up with it; and as they assert that the restoration of a thing once destroyed to existence is unthinkable, they deny the immortality of the soul. Consequently they deny heaven, hell, resurrection, and judgment. Acknowledging neither a recompense for good deeds nor a punishment for evil ones, they fling

off all authority and plunge into sensual pleasures with the avidity of brutes. These also ought to be called atheists, for the true faith depends not only on the acknowledgment of God, but of His Apostle and of the Day of Judgment. And although they acknowledge God and His attributes, they deny a judgment to come.

(3) Next come the *Theists*. Among them should be reckoned Socrates, who was the teacher of Plato as Plato was of Aristotle. This latter drew up for his disciples the rules of logic, organised the sciences, elucidated what was formerly obscure, and expounded what had not been understood. This school refuted the systems of the two others, i.e., the Materialists and Naturalists.

When I had finished my examination of these doctrines I applied myself to the study of Sufism. I saw that in order to understand it thoroughly one must combine theory with practice. The aim which the Sufis set before them is as follows: To free the soul from the tyrannical yoke of the passions, to deliver it from its wrong inclinations and evil instincts, in order that in the purified heart there should only remain room for God and for the invocation of His holy name.

As it was more easy to learn their doctrine than to practise it, I studied first of all those of their books which contain it: *The Nourishment of Hearts*, by Abu Talib of Mecca, the works of Hareth el Muhasibi, and the fragments which still remain of Junaid, Shibli, Abu Yezid Bustami and other leaders (whose souls may God sanctify). I acquired a thorough knowledge of their researches, and I learned all that was possible to learn of their methods by study and oral teaching. It became clear to me that the last stage could not be reached by mere instruction, but only by transport, ecstasy, and the transformation of the moral being.

I saw that Sufism consists in experiences rather than in definitions, and that what I was lacking belonged to the domain, not of instruction, but of ecstasy and initiation.

Examining my actions, the most fair-seeming of which were my lecturing and professorial occupations, I found to my surprise that I was engrossed in several studies of little value, and profitless as regards my salvation. I probed the motives of my teaching and found that, in place of being sincerely consecrated to God, it was only actuated by a vain desire of honour and reputation.

In these reflections I spent a long time. Still a prey to uncertainty, one day I decided to leave Bagdad and to give up everything; the next day I gave up my resolution. I advanced one step and immediately relapsed. In the morning I was sincerely resolved only to occupy myself with the future life; in the evening a crowd of carnal thoughts assailed and dispersed my resolutions. On the one side the world kept me bound to my post in the chains of covetousness, on the other side the voice of religion cried to me, "Up! Up! thy life is nearing its end, and thou hast a long journey to make. All thy pretended knowledge is nought but falsehood and fantasy. If thou dost not think now of thy salvation, when wilt thou think of it? If thou dost not break thy chains to-day, when wilt thou break them?" Then my resolve was strengthened, I wished to give up all and flee; but the Tempter, returning to the attack, said, "You are suffering from a transitory feeling; don't give way to it, for it will soon pass. If you obey it, if you give up this fine position, this honourable post exempt from trouble and rivalry, this seat of authority safe from attack, you will regret it later on without being able to recover it."

Thus I remained, torn asunder by the opposite forces of earthly passions and religious aspirations, for about six months from the month Rajab of the year A.D. 1096. At the close of them my will yielded and I gave myself up to destiny. God caused an impediment to chain my tongue and prevented me from lecturing. Vainly I desired, in the interest of my pupils, to go on with my teaching, but my mouth became dumb. The silence to which I was condemned cast me into a violent despair; my stomach became weak; I lost all appetite; I could neither swallow a morsel of bread nor drink a drop of water.

The enfeeblement of my physical powers was such that the doctors, despairing of saving me, said, "The mischief is in the heart, and has communicated itself to the whole organism; there is no hope unless the cause of his grievous sadness be arrested."

Finally, conscious of my weakness and the prostration of my soul, I took refuge in God as a man at the end of himself and without resources. "He who hears the wretched when they cry" (Koran xxvii:63) deigned to hear me; He made easy to me the sacrifice of honours, wealth, and family. I gave out publicly that I intended to make the pilgrimage to Mecca, while I secretly resolved to go to Syria, not wishing that the Caliph (may God magnify him) or my friends should know my intention of settling in that country. I made all kinds of clever excuses for leaving Bagdad with the fixed intention of not returning thither. The Imāms of Irak criticised me with one accord. Not one of them could admit that this sacrifice had a religious motive, because they considered my position as the highest attainable in the religious community. "Behold how far their knowledge goes!" (Koran liii:31). All kinds of explanations of my conduct were forthcoming. Those who were outside the limits of Irak attributed it to the fear with which the Government inspired me. Those who were on the spot and saw how the authorities wished to detain me, their displeasure at my resolution and my refusal of their request, said to themselves, "It is a calamity which one can only impute to a fate which has befallen the Faithful and Learning!"

At last I left Bagdad, giving up all my fortune. Only, as lands and property in Irak can afford an endowment for pious purposes, I obtained a legal authorisation to preserve as much as was necessary for my support and that of my children; for there is surely nothing more lawful in the world than that a learned man should provide sufficient to support his family. I then betook myself to Syria, where I remained for two years, which I devoted to retirement, meditation, and devout exercises. I only thought of self-improvement and discipline and of purification of the heart by prayer in going through the forms of devotion which the Sufis had taught me. I used to live a solitary life in the Mosque of Damascus, and was in the habit of spending my days on the minaret after closing the door behind me.

From thence I proceeded to Jerusalem, and every day secluded myself in the Sanctuary of the Rock. After that I felt a desire to accomplish the Pilgrimage, and to receive a full effusion of grace by visiting Mecca, Medina, and the Tomb of the Prophet. After visiting the shrine of the Friend of God (Abraham), I went to the Hedjāz. Finally, the longings of my heart and the prayers of my children brought me back to my country, although I was so firmly resolved at first never to revisit it. At any rate I meant, if I did return, to live there solitary and in religious meditation; but events, family cares, and vicissitudes of life changed my resolutions and troubled my meditative calm. However irregular the intervals which I could give to devotional ecstasy, my confidence in it did not diminish; and the more I was diverted by hindrances, the more steadfastly I returned to it.

Ten years passed in this manner. During my successive periods of meditation there were revealed to me things impossible to recount. All that I shall say for the edification of the reader is this: I learnt from a sure source that the Sufis are the true pioneers on the path of God; that there is nothing more beautiful than their life, nor more praiseworthy than their rule of conduct, nor purer than their morality. The intelligence of thinkers, the wisdom of philosophers, the knowledge of the most learned doctors of the law would in vain combine their efforts in order to modify or improve their doctrine and morals; it would be impossible. With the Sufis, repose and movement, exterior or interior, are illumined with the light which proceeds from the Central Radiance of Inspiration. And what other light could shine on the face of the earth? In a word, what can one criticise in them? To purge the heart of all that does not belong to God is the first step in their cathartic method. The drawing up of the heart by prayer is the keystone of it, as the cry "Allahu Akbar" (God is great) is the keystone of prayer, and the last stage is the being lost in God. I say the last stage, with reference to what may be reached by an effort of will; but, to tell the truth, it is only the first stage in the life of contemplation, the vestibule by which the initiated enter.

From the time that they set out on this path, revelations commence for them. They come to see in the waking state angels and souls of prophets; they hear their voices and wise counsels. By means of this contemplation of heavenly forms and images they rise by degrees to heights which human language cannot reach, which one cannot even indicate without falling into great and inevitable errors. The degree of proximity to Deity which they attain is regarded by some as intermixture of being (*haloul*), by others as identification (*ittihād*), by others as intimate union (*wasl*). But all these expressions are wrong, as have explained in our work entitled *The Chief Aim*. Those who have reached that stage should confine themselves to repeating the verse—

What I experience I shall not try to say;
Call me happy, but ask me no more.

In short, he who does not arrive at the intuition of these truths by means of ecstasy, knows only the *name* of inspiration. The miracles wrought by the saints are, in fact, merely the earliest forms of prophetic manifestation. Such was the state of the Apostle of God when, before receiving his commission, he retired to Mount Hira to give himself up to such intensity of prayer and meditation that the Arabs said: "Muhammed is become enamoured of God."

From other Sufis:

> In the school of Divine Truth, as you learn from the teachers of Love, strive in every way, my son, so that one day you may become a father in wisdom. . . . If the radiance of the love of God falls on your heart and soul, surely you will become fairer than the sun in the firmament. Rid yourself of the copper of your own self, like the warriors of the Path, so that you may find the alchemy of Love and become gold. The light of God will shine on you, enveloping you from head to foot, when you are born without head and foot along the Path of the All-Glorious. For one moment sink into the ocean of God, and do not suppose that one hair of your head shall be moistened by the water of the seven seas. If the vision you behold is the Face of God, there is no doubt that from this time forward you will see clearly. When the foundations of your own existence are destroyed, have no fear in your heart that you yourself will perish. O Hafiz, if in thine heart, thou dost crave for union, thou wilt need to become as the dust on the threshold of those who contemplate the Vision of God.

———Hafiz (1320–1390)

At the beginning I was mistaken in four respects. I concerned myself to remember God, to know Him, to love Him and to seek Him. When I had come to the end I saw that He had remembered me before I remembered Him, that His knowledge of me had preceded my knowledge of Him, His love towards me had existed before my love to Him and He had sought me before I sought Him.

I thought that I had arrived at the very Throne of God and I said to it, "O Throne, they tell us that God rests upon thee." "O Bayazid," replied the Throne, "we are told here that He dwells in a humble heart."

For thirty years God Most High was my mirror, now I am my own mirror and that which I was I am no more. . . . Behold, now I say that God is the mirror of myself, for with my tongue He speaks and I have passed away.

————Bayazid Al-Bistami (died A.D. 877)

For you there is an ascent of the soul towards the Divine Light, therefore shall your heart and soul in the end attain to union with that Light. With your whole heart and soul, seek to regain Reality, nay, seek for Reality within your own heart, for Reality, in truth, is hidden within you. The heart is the dwelling-place of that which is the Essence of the universe, within the heart and soul is the very Essence of God. Like the saints, make a journey into your self; like the lovers of God, cast one glance within. As a lover now, in contemplation of the Beloved, be unveiled within and behold the Essence. Form is a veil to you, and your heart is a veil. When the veil vanishes, you will become all light.

Tear aside the veils of all you see in this world and you will find yourself apart in solitude with God. If you draw aside the veils of the stars and the spheres, you will see that all is one with the Essence of your own pure soul. If you will but tear aside the veil, you will become pure, as He is pure. Cast aside the veil from existence and non-existence and you will see forthwith the true meaning of God's purpose.

———Farid al-Din Attar (1142–1220)

7

THE SHEKHINAH

לֹא־יִהְיֶה־לָּךְ
עוֹד הַשֶּׁמֶשׁ לְאוֹר יוֹמָם
וּלְנֹגַהּ הַיָּרֵחַ לֹא־יָאִיר לָךְ
וְהָיָה־לָךְ יְהֹוָה לְאוֹר עוֹלָם
וֵאלֹהַיִךְ לְתִפְאַרְתֵּךְ׃

The sun shall be no more thy
    light by day,
Neither for brightness shall
    the moon give light unto
    thee;
But the Lord shall be unto
    thee an everlasting light,
And thy God thy glory.

————Isaiah 60:19

♦ ♦ ♦

Orthodox Judaism is a religion deeply committed to the *written* word. The ten commandments were not only revealed to Moses, they were written in stone. All private and public life is dictated by written Law. To read the sacred books, the Torah and the Talmud, is in itself an act of worship. "It is written," is the sounding cry of the devout Jew. But quite apart from the written law, there exists a mystic side to Judaism, known as the Kabbalah. From the start, the Kabbalah was denounced by orthodox rabbis and existed only as a secret, underground fraternity. For centuries there were very few books on the Kabbalah; what writings did exist were couched in obscure symbolism in order to protect the secret knowledge and those who followed it. But then, in a Jewish community of 13th-century Spain, there appeared a new and startling book. This book revealed like never before the secret knowledge of the Kabbalists and their most prized treasure, the Shekhinah.

♦ ♦ ♦

In 1291, the land of Israel was subjected to another foreign invasion of its territory. The Israeli city of Acre was hard hit and most of its Jewish and Christian inhabitants were massacred. One of its citizens, a young Jew named Isaac ben Samuel, managed to escape and flee to Spain. Arriving in Toledo, the young man was quickly accepted into the Jewish community flourishing there at that time. Soon, Isaac began to hear reports of a marvelous new book being quietly circulated within the community. Its title was Zohar, a word meaning "brightness," and taken from a verse in Daniel: "And they that be wise shall shine as the brightness of the firmament" (Daniel 12:3). The book had only recently appeared, but its origins were ancient. It had been written in Israel hundreds of years previously and it recounted the adventures and sayings of the great second century wise man, Rabbi Shim'on.

Now Isaac of Acre had certainly heard of Rabbi Shim'on, who was widely venerated back in Israel as a great interpreter of the Talmud, but he had never before heard of this wonderful book of his teachings. The book was being dispersed in a series of small booklets by a certain Spanish Jew, Moses de Leon. They were written in Aramaic, the ancient language of the Hebrews, now all but forgotten in 13th-century Spain. The booklets not only gave generous account of Rabbi Shim'on's amazing adventures, but illucidated the long-held secrets of Jewish mysticism like never before. Isaac determined to meet this Moses de Leon in person and to see for himself the original manuscript.

True to his intent, Isaac at last met with Moses de Leon in the city of Valladolid, and the old man agreed to show him the manuscript. It was, de Leon said, back in his home town of Avila, and the two soon embarked for that city. But disaster struck and Moses de Leon died en route homeward. Undeterred, Isaac continued the journey, still intent on seeing the original Zohar manuscript.

Arriving in Avila, Isaac was directed to the home of de Leon's widow. His interview with her was shocking. She informed him that there never was an original ancient manuscript. Isaac's diary quotes her as saying: "He wrote it entirely from his own head . . . I saw him writing with nothing in front of him."

Isaac never was able to determine the truth of the Zohar's authorship and it remained a mystery for centuries. Moses de Leon, the original distributor, was in time forgotten and the Zohar became widely accepted as an authentic book of Rabbi Shim'on's teachings from the second century. As such, it became the classic par excellence of Jewish mysticism. Occasionally, a scholar would point out certain anachronisms and other clues that indicated the book could not have originated in the second century. But it was not until the dedicated research of Gershom Scholem in the 1920's that the authorship of the Zohar was firmly established as the work of Moses de Leon of the 13th century.

De Leon's reasons for claiming an ancient source for his own writing can only be guessed at. Certainly the book's supposed antiquity and the famous name of Rabbi Shim'on garnered immediate interest in the book. There have been those who have attributed totally selfish motives for De Leon's forgery, while some modern students of the Zohar have put forth the theory that De Leon may have sincerely felt himself possessed by a power beyond his own in writing the work, as evidenced by certain points: it is literally a vast work, usually printed in three to five thick volumes, but was composed in a few years' time. It is written in Aramaic (the native tongue of Rabbi Shim'on, which de Leon knew only from his study of two books). Many passages exude a transcendent enthusiasm which bespeaks a deep, trance-like writing. The style shows many characteristics of the psychic technique of automatic writing, a technique used by other Jewish mystic writers. It is noted that de Leon's other writings, all in Hebrew, were of a decidedly different style. Certain modern scholars, far from condemning de Leon's method, attribute the Zohar's greatness to the freedom of expression allowed by de Leon's adoption of a literary alter-ego.

Whatever de Leon's methods and motivations in composing the Zohar, it remains the unqualified apex of Jewish mystical literature. For Jewish mystics, it has attained equal status with the Torah itself. Its "spiritual novel" of Rabbi Shim'on's adventures unveils for the reader the long-kept secrets of the Jewish mystic path.

Before the Zohar, Jewish mystics had been reluctant to publicly disclose any personal details of their lives and experiences. What teachings these men had left behind were collected and known as the Kabbalah. The writings of the Kabbalists were typically veiled in almost impenetrable symbolism. An initial perusal of Kabbalistic literature usually uncovers little more than a bewildering array of magic codes, numerology, and a bizarre juggling of the Hebrew alphabet. But the Zohar, and later writings, at last revealed the true heart and goal of Jewish mysticism: the *Shekhinah*, the indwelling divine light.

According to the Zohar, the light of the infinite God is so splendorous that no man can see it and live. This light permeates every animate and inanimate object of the universe but its reality surpasses all human comprehension. Even the great Jewish patriarchs Abraham, Moses, and Ezekiel could only absorb a portion of this splendor. The light of God, in its infinite expression, is known as the *Ain Sof.* From this light eminate ten lesser lights by which the materialized world comes into being. Each of these ten lights are given a number of elaborate appellations and symbolic attributes. The tenth and least of these lights is the Shekhinah. It is this light, the indwelling spirit of God in human beings, that can be perceived and enjoyed by individual people. From the Zohar is this description of the ten lights:

> The Most Ancient One is at the same time the most Hidden of the hidden. He is separated from all things, and is at the same time not separated from all things. For all things are united in Him, and He unites Himself with all things. There is nothing which is not in Him. He has a shape, and one can say that He has not one. In assuming a shape, He has given existence to all things. He made ten lights spring forth from His midst, lights

which shine with the form which they have borrowed from Him, and which shed everywhere the
light of a brilliant day. The Ancient One, the most
Hidden of the hidden, is a high beacon, and we
know Him only by His lights, which illuminate
our eyes so abundantly. His Holy Name is no
other thing than these lights.[1]

The overriding concern of the Zohar is the attainment of
the Shekhinah in the individual life of the devotee. In the
book, Rabbi Shim'on and his followers travel throughout
Israel, strengthened and inspired by their study of the
Torah and their great yearning for the Shekhinah. But the
Shekhinah is deeply hidden and must be yearned for with
a passion no less intense than the passion of sexual desire.
This requirement is stressed by Elizah de Vidas, a 15th-
century interpreter of the Zohar:

Cleaving to God consists in a person's attaching
himself with his soul to the Shekhinah and con-
centrating all his attention upon Her unification,
as well as upon separating all the evil shells from
Her. . . . A person should cleave to the Shekhinah
with his soul by means of each and every com-
mandment that he performs; he must carry them
out with longing, heartfelt enthusiasm and very
great love. This is what is intended by the quality
of "desire of the heart" of which the Zohar frequently speaks. It is not possible to attain such
desire of the heart—which is what this longing is—
unless a person initially sets his mind on God,
may He be blessed, and upon the love which he
feels for him. . . . Just as an individual who longs
for the one whom he loves eliminates all other

[1]J. Abelson, *Jewish Mysticism: An Introduction to the Kabbalah* (London, 1913; reprinted New York: Sepher-Hermon Press, Inc., 1981), pp. 136, 137.

thoughts from his mind because of his preoccupa-
tion with his lover, a fire of love burns in his heart
even while he eats, drinks and sleeps, so should a
person's love for God be likewise. We learn this
from a story told by Rabbi Isaac of Acre. Among
the stories having to do with ascetics which this
sage reported, he wrote that a person who has
never experienced longing for a woman is like a
donkey—even worse. The reason for this is that as
a result of the feeling of longing for a woman, one
learns to cultivate longing for God. We can learn
from this that the man who loves the Torah with
such great passion that he thinks of no worldly
matters whatsoever, neither by day nor by night,
will assuredly attain to a most wonderful grade of
soul.[2]

In the Zohar, the presence of the Shekhinah is experienced by Rabbi Shim'on and his followers in varying
degrees, but it is at the death of Rabbi Shim'on that the
Shekhinah finally makes its presence clearly manifested.
This passage from the Zohar is entitled "The Wedding
Celebration" as the death of the great Rabbi is seen as a
marriage to the divine. The ecstatic tone of this passage is
typical of the Zohar and explains some of the inspirational
power this book has held for so many Jewish mystics.

On the day that Rabbi Shim'on
was to leave the world,
while he was arranging his affairs,
the Comrades assembled at his house.
Present were Rabbi El'azar,
his son, Rabbi Abba,

---

[2]Barry W. Holtz, *Back to the Sources*, copyright © 1984 Barry W. Holtz (New York:
Simon and Schuster, 1984), pp. 347, 349, 351. Reprinted by permission of Simon
and Schuster, New York.

and the other Comrades.
The house was full.
Rabbi Shim'on raised his eyes and saw
that the house was filled.
He cried, and said
"The other time I was ill,
Rabbi Pinhas son of Ya'ir
was in my presence.
I was already selecting my place in Paradise . . .
When I returned,
fire was whirling in front of me;
it has never gone out.
No human has entered without permission.
Now I see that it has gone out,
and the house is filled!"

While they were sitting
Rabbi Shim'on opened his eyes
and saw what he saw;
fire whirled through the house.
Rabbi Shim'on rose and laughed in delight.

Rabbi Abba sat behind him
and Rabbi El'azar in front.
Rabbi Shim'on said,
"Now is a time of favor!
I want to enter without shame
into the world that is coming.
Holy words, until now unrevealed,
I want to reveal
in the presence of Shekhinah;
so it will not be said
that I left the world deficiently.
Until now they were hidden in my heart
as a password to the world that is coming.
I will arrange you like this:

Rabbi Abba will write;
Rabbi El'azar, my son, will repeat;
the other Comrades will meditate within."

Rabbi Shim'on said
"In the threshing house,
we were found to be:
all the Comrades speaking, I among them.
Now I alone will speak;
all are listening to my words,
those above and those below.
Happy is my portion this day!"

Rabbi Shim'on opened and said
" 'I am my Beloved's,
his desire is upon me'
(Song of Songs 7:11).
All the days that I have been bound
to this world
I have been bound
in a single bond with the Blessed Holy One.
That is why now 'His desire is upon me'!
He and His holy company
have come to hear in joy concealed words
and praise for the Holy Ancient One,
Concealed of all Concealed!
Separate, separated from all,
yet not separate!
For all is attached to It,
and It is attached to all.
It is all!
Ancient of all Ancients!
Concealed of all Concealed!
Arrayed and not arrayed.
Arrayed in order to sustain all;
not arrayed, for It is not to be found.

When arrayed, It generates nine lights,
flaming from It, from Its array.
Those lights, sparkling, flashing,
radiate, emenate to all sides.

Until now these words were concealed,
for I was scared to reveal;
now they have been revealed!
Yet it is revealed before the Holy Ancient One
that I have not acted for my own honor
nor for the honor of my family
but rather so I will not enter
his palace in shame.
Furthermore, I see that the Blessed Holy One
and all these righteous ones approve:
I see all of them rejoicing in this,
my wedding celebration!
Happy is my portion!"

Rabbi Abba said
"When the Holy Spark,
the High Spark, finished this word
he raised his hands and cried and laughed.
He wanted to reveal one word.
He said, 'I have been troubled
by this word all my days
and now they are not giving me permission!
I have seen that all those sparks
sparkle from the High Spark,
Hidden of all Hidden!
All are levels of enlightenment.
In the light of each and every level
there is revealed what is revealed.
All those lights are connected:
this light to that light,
that light to this light,

one shining into the other,
inseparable, one from the other.

The light of each and every spark,
called Adornments of the King,
Crowns of the King—
each one shines into, joins onto
the light within, within,
not separating without.
So all rises to one level,
all is crowned with one word;
no separating one from the other.
It and Its Name is one.

The light that is revealed
is called the Garment of the King.
The light within,
within is a concealed light.
In that light dwells the Ineffable one,
the Unrevealed.
All those sparks and all those lights
sparkle from the Holy Ancient One,
Concealed of all Concealed,
the High Spark.
Upon reflecting,
all those lights emanating—
there is nothing but the High Spark,
hidden and unrevealed! . . . ' "

Rabbi Abba said
"Before the Holy Spark finished . . .
his words subsided.
I was still writing,
intending to write more
but I heard nothing.
I did not raise my head:

the light was overwhelming;
I could not look.
Then I started trembling.
I heard a voice calling:
'Length of days and years of life . . . '
(Proverbs 3:2).
I heard another voice:
'He asked You for life . . . '
(Psalms 21:5).

All day long, the fire
in the house did not go out.
No one reached him; no one could:
light and fire surrounded him!
All day long, I lay on the ground and wailed.
After the fire disappeared
I saw the Holy Spark,
Holy of Holies, leaving the world,
enwrapped, lying on his right,
his face smiling."

Happy is his portion above and below![3]

Despite the reluctance of Jewish mystics to disclose personal details of their own lives and experiences, the Jewish mystical tradition does contain a few examples of the type of spiritual autobiography collected for the other tales of this anthology. Concluding this chapter on the Shekhinah is one such personal account, from the diary of the Jewish Kabbalist, Rabbi Isaac Eizik of Komarno (1806–1874).

---

[3]Daniel C. Matt, trans., *Zohar: The Book of Enlightenment*, Classics of Western Spirituality series, copyright © 1983 Daniel C. Matt (Mahwah, NJ: Paulist Press, 1983), pp. 182, 183, 184. Used by permission of Paulist Press, Mahwah, NJ, and by permission of The Society for Promoting Christian Knowledge, London.

◆ ◆ ◆

At the age of sixteen I married my true partner. She belonged to the ru'ah ("spirit") aspect of my soul but since I myself had not attained as yet to the ru'ah aspect there were many obstacles to the match. However, thanks to the power of my repentance and industry in studying the Torah, no stranger passed between us. After this I attained to many lofty stages of the holy spirit, the result of my industry in Torah study and in divine worship. The truth be told, I did not appreciate at the time that it was not the result of my own efforts since I was still remote from true worship. But after reflecting on the matter I separated myself entirely from the world. It happened in the year 5583 (= 1823) at the beginning of winter. My special room was so cold that it had not been heated even once during the whole of the winter. It was my habit to sleep only two hours a day, spending the rest of the time studying the Torah, the Talmud, the Codes, the Zohar, the writings of our Master (Isaac Luria) and the works of Rabbi Moses Cordovero. But I fell away from all these stages and for three months was in a state of immense smallness of soul. Many harsh and demonic forces (kelippot) rose against me to dissuade me from studying the Torah. Worse than all was the state of melancholy into which I was hurled. Yet my heart was as firm as a rock. During this time the only pleasure I allowed myself was to drink a little water and eat a morsel of bread daily. I had no delight whatever in the Torah I studied or the prayers I recited. The cold was very severe and the demonic forces extremely powerful so that I actually stood equally balanced between two paths, depending on how I would choose. Much bitterness passed over my head as a result of these blandishments, really more bitter than a thousand times death. But once I had overcome these blandishments, suddenly, in the midst of the day, as I was studying tractate Yevamot in the name of the eternal God, in order to adorn the Shekhinah with all my might, a great light fell upon me. The whole house became filled with light, a marvelous light, the Shekhinah resting there. This was the first time in my life that I had some little taste of His light, may He be blessed. It was authentic without error or confusion, a wondrous delight and a most pleasant illumination beyond all comprehension. From that time onwards I began to serve the Creator of all with a marvelous, unvarying illumination. The blandishments had power over me no longer. Afterwards I fell once again for a time so I came to realize that I must journey to the saints who would draw down His light, blessed be He, upon me since I already had a refined vessel wherewith to receive the light.[4]

[4]Lewis Jacobs, *Jewish Mystical Testimonies* (Jerusalem: Keter Publishing House Ltd., copyright © 1976), pp. 240, 241. Reprinted by permission of Schocken Books, published by Pantheon Books, a division of Random House, Inc., and by permission of Keter Publishing House Ltd., Jerusalem.

8

THE PRAYER OF QUIET

Si estuviera muchos años imaginando cómo figurar cosa tan hermosa, no pudiera ni supiera, porque excede a todo lo que acá se puede imaginar, aun sola la blancura y resplandor. No es resplandor que deslumbre, sino una blancura suave, y el resplandor infuso.

If I were to spend years and years imagining how to invent anything so beautiful, I could not do it, and I do not even know how I should try, for, even in its whiteness and radiance alone, it exceeds all that we can imagine. It is not a radiance which dazzles, but a soft whiteness and an infused radiance.

————St. Teresa of Avila,
The Book of Her Life

The tale within this chapter is a gathering of passages from the following sources:

St. Teresa of Avila, *The Life of Teresa of Jesus*, translated and edited by E. Allison Peers (New York: Doubleday and Company, Inc., 1960), from chapters 1–8, 10, 13, 18, 20, 28. Used by kind permission of Sheed and Ward.

"The Way of Perfection," from Volume II of *The Complete Works of Saint Teresa of Jesus*, translated and edited by E. Allison Peers (New York: Sheed and Ward, Inc., 1946), from chapters 31 and 28. Used by kind permission.

Teresa of Avila: The Interior Castle, translated by Kieran Kavanaugh, OCD and Otilio Rodriguez, OCD, copyright © 1979 The Washington Province of Discalced Carmelites, Inc., pp. 36, 133, 135–136, 141–143. Used by kind permission of Paulist Press, Mahwah, NJ.

♦ ♦ ♦

Around the year 1560, rumors were flying in the central Spanish town of Avila regarding an inhabitant of the nearby Monastery of the Incarnation. The object of these rumors was a young nun, Teresa de Cepeda y Ahumada. It was told that she had visions and enjoyed mysterious divine favors. But many people, including the nun's own confessor, were convinced these raptures and visions were the work of the devil. It was further claimed that Teresa was secretly a member of the Alumbrados, a religious sect who claimed direct enlightenment by the Holy Spirit, independent of the Church. The Alumbrados were being tried by the Spanish Inquisition as heretics and enemies of the Faith and many believed that Teresa should likewise be put on trial.

Teresa's confessions were heard by a great number of priests. Some commanded her to resist the visions while a few others encouraged her and became her staunch allies. Teresa herself was overwhelmed with self-doubt and the constant fear of being misunderstood. Finally, a new confessor, P. Ibáñez, commanded her to put down in writing a clear, complete account of both her life history and her interior experiences.

Teresa obediently set to work on "her book." Lacking any formal training as a writer, she wrote in the vernacular Spanish rather than the literary Latin. Her writing is informal and colloquial, entirely without paragraphs or punctuation. As directed, she was completely candid in regard to her life events and especially her spiritual experiences. The work was slow, as Teresa had to steal stray moments from her structured schedule in order to write. Soon though, her circumstances altered drastically. The richest woman of the great city of Toledo had lost a child and was overwrought with grief. This woman, Doña Luisa de la Cerda, having heard the rumors of the "saint" of Avila, requested the nun's presence in her own home. Accordingly, Teresa was sent to Toledo and indeed proved to be of great consolation to the grieving mother. In the truly luxurious quarters provided her in Doña Luisa's house, Teresa was able to dedicate much time to her book and she completed the manuscript in June 1562.

Returning to the convent in Avila, Teresa enjoyed a period of five tranquil years, the most peaceful of her life. But her trials resumed. Her book became widely circulated among Dominican theologians, secular priests and lay people. In the summer of 1569, a copy of the book was lent to the Princess of Éboli, Doña Ana de Mendoza. The princess denounced the work and submitted it to the courts of the Spanish Inquisition. Eventually the official examination proved wholly in the book's favor and Teresa was allowed to begin her lifetime work of reform of the Carmelite convents of Spain, although this work and Teresa's life continued to provoke controversy throughout her lifetime. On two more occasions she was commanded by her superiors to write. *The Way of Perfection* and *The Interior Castle* took up the teachings begun in her autobiography.

Teresa's principal task in all her writings is to explain what she means by, and experiences in, "mental prayer." She usually calls this prayer by the name "Prayer of Quiet," which further deepens into the "Prayer of Union." Mental prayer, for Teresa, is distinguished from the "vocal prayer commonly practiced by all," and has much obviously in common with the meditation practices of other spiritual disciplines.

During her lifetime, and continually till the present, Teresa's books have delighted countless readers. Her lack of grammatical style does not diminish the clarity she achieves in discussing the deepest aspects of interior states of consciousness, a subject always resistant to verbal expression. Had Teresa not been commanded to write by her spiritual directors, the on-going tradition of the inner light would have sadly lacked this very significant feminine voice. The following tale is a gathering of passages principally taken from Teresa's first work, *The Book of Her Life*, and briefly from her two later works.

◆ ◆ ◆

My father was fond of reading good books and had some in Spanish so that his children might read them too. These books, together with the care which my mother took to make us say our prayers and to lead us to be devoted to Our Lady and to certain saints, began to awaken good desires in me when I was, I suppose, about six or seven years old. My father was a man of great charity towards the poor, who was good to the sick and also to his servants—so much so that he could never be brought to keep slaves, because of his compassion for them. On one occasion, when he had a slave of a brother of his in the house, he was as good to her as to his own children. He used to say that it caused him intolerable distress that she was not free. He was strictly truthful: nobody ever heard him swear or speak evil.

My mother, too, was a very virtuous woman, who endured a life of great infirmity. Though extremely beautiful, she was never known to give any reason for supposing that she made the slightest account of her beauty; and, though she died at thirty-three, her dress was already that of a person advanced in years.

I remember that, when my mother died, I was twelve years of age or a little less. When I began to realize what I had lost, I went in my distress to an image of Our Lady and with many tears besought her to be a mother to me. Though I did this in my simplicity, I believe it was of some avail to me. I was taken to a convent in the place where I lived, in which children like myself were being educated. Now, as my sister had married, and I had no mother, I should have been alone in the house if I had not gone there, which would not have been fitting.

At first I was very restless; but within a week, perhaps even earlier, I was much happier than I had been in my father's house. Although at that time I had the greatest possible aversion to being a nun, I was very pleased to see nuns who were so good; for in that house they were all very good. There was a nun who slept with those of us who were seculars and it was through her that the Lord seems to have been pleased to begin to give me light. As I began to enjoy the good and holy conversation of this nun, I grew to delight in listening to her, for she spoke well about God and was very discreet and holy. There was never a time, I think, when I did not delight in listening to her words.

I remained in this convent for a year and a half, and was much the better for it. I began to say a great many vocal prayers. But I was still anxious not to be a nun, for God had not as yet been pleased to give me this desire, although I was also afraid of marriage. At this time, though I was not careless about my own improvement, the Lord sent me a serious illness, which forced me to return to my father's house. When I got better, they took me to see my sister, who was living in a village. She was so fond of me that, if she had had her way, I should never have left her. Her husband was also very fond of me—at least, he showed me every kindness.

On the road leading to my sister's lived one of my father's brothers, a widower, who was a very shrewd man and full of virtues. He wanted me to stay with him for some days. It was his practice to read good books in Spanish and his conversation was ordinarily about God and the vanity of the world. Though I stayed here for only a few days, such was the impression made on my heart by the words of God, both as read and as heard, and the excellence of my uncle's company, that I began to understand the truth, which I had learned as a child, that all things are nothing, and that the world is vanity and will soon pass away. I began to fear that, if I had died of my illness, I should have gone to hell; and though, even then, I could not incline my will to being a nun, I saw that this was the best and safest state, and so, little by little, I determined to force myself to embrace it. This decision, then, to enter the religious life seems to have been inspired by servile fear more than by love.

The fact that I had now become fond of good books gave me new life. I would read the epistles of Saint Jerome; and these inspired me with such courage that I determined to tell my father of my decision, which was going almost as far as taking the habit. He was so fond of me that I was never able to get his consent, nor did the requests of persons whom I asked to speak with him about it succeed in doing so. The most I could obtain from him was permission to do as I liked after his death. As I distrusted myself and thought I might turn back out of weakness, this course seemed an unsuitable one. So I achieved my aim in another way, as I shall now explain.

During this time, when I was considering these resolutions, I had persuaded one of my brothers, by talking to him about the vanity of the world, to become a friar, and we agreed to set out together, very early one morning, for the convent. In making my final decision, I had already resolved that I would go to any convent in which I thought I could serve God better or which my father might wish me to enter. I remember—and I really believe this is true—that when I left my father's house my distress was so great that I do not think it will be greater when I die. It seemed to me as if every bone in my body were being wrenched asunder; for, as I had no love of God to subdue my love for my father and kinsfolk, everything was such a strain to me that, if the Lord had not helped me, no reflections of my own would have sufficed to keep me true to my purpose. But the Lord gave me courage to fight against myself and so I carried out my intention. When I took the habit, there came to me a new joy, which amazed me, for I could not understand whence it arose.

The change in my life, and in my diet, affected my health; and though my happiness was great, it was not sufficient to cure me. I suffered so much from heart trouble that everyone who saw me was alarmed. I also had many other ailments. I spent my first year, therefore, in a very poor state of health. My condition became so serious—for I hardly ever seemed to be fully conscious, and sometimes I lost consciousness altogether—that my father made great efforts to find me a cure. As our own doctors could suggest none, he arranged for me to be taken to a place where they had a great reputation for curing other kinds of illness and said they could also cure mine. On the way there, I stopped at the house of this uncle of mine, which, as I have said, was on the road, and he gave me a book called *Third Alphabet*, which treats of the Prayer of Recollection. During this first year I had been reading good books, but I did not know how to practise prayer, or how to recollect myself, and so I was delighted with the book and determined to follow that way of prayer with all my might. I began to spend periods in solitude, to go frequently to confession and to start upon the way of prayer with this book for my guide. For I found no other guide (no confessor, I mean) who understood me, though I sought one for fully twenty years subsequently to the time I am speaking of.

My treatment was to commence at the beginning of the summer and I had left the convent when the winter began. All the intervening time I spent in the house of the sister whom I referred to above as living in a village, waiting for the month of April. I remained in that place [of treatment] for three months suffering the greatest trials, for the treatment was more drastic than my constitution could stand. At the end of two months, the severity of the remedies had almost ended my life, and the pain in my heart, which I had gone there to get treated, was much worse; sometimes I felt as if sharp teeth had hold of me, and so severe was the pain they caused that it was feared I was going mad. My strength suffered a grave decline, for I could take nothing but liquid, had a great distaste for food, was in a continual fever, and became so wasted away that, after they had given me purgatives daily for almost a month, I was, as it were, so shrivelled up that my nerves began to shrink. These symptoms were accompanied by intolerable pain which gave me no rest by night or by day. Altogether I was in a state of great misery.

Seeing that I had gained nothing here, my father took me away and once again called in the doctors. They all gave me up, saying that, quite apart from everything else, I was consumptive. And now the August festival of Our Lady came round. I had been in torment ever since April, though the last three months were the worst. I hastened to go to confession, for I was always very fond of frequent confession. That night I had a fit, which left me unconscious for nearly four days. During that time they gave me the Sacrament of Unction, and from hour to hour, from moment to moment, thought I was dying; they did nothing but repeat the Creed to me, as though I could have understood any of it. There must have been times when they were sure I was dead, for afterwards I actually found some wax on my eyelids. My father was in great distress. Many cries and prayers were made for me to God. Blessed be He Who was pleased to hear them! For a day and a half there was an open grave in my convent, where they were awaiting my body, and in one of the monasteries of our Order, some way from here, they had performed the rites for the dead. But it pleased the Lord that I should return to consciousness.

After this fit, which lasted for four days, I was in such a state that only the Lord can know what intolerable sufferings I experienced. My only alleviation was that, if no one came near me, my pains often ceased; and when I had rested a little I used to think I was getting well. I was now so eager to return to the convent that they had me taken there. So, instead of the dead body they had expected, the nuns received a living soul. I remained in this condition for more than eight months, and my paralysis, though it kept improving, continued for nearly three years. When I began to get about on my hands and knees, I praised God. All this I bore with great resignation, and, except at the beginning, with great joy; for none of it could compare with the pains and torments which I had suffered at first.

I began, then, to indulge in one pastime after another, in one vanity after another. So far was my soul led astray by all these vanities, that I was ashamed to return to God and to approach Him in the intimate friendship which comes from prayer. I began to be afraid to pray. It seemed to me better to live like everyone else; to recite, vocally, the prayers that I was bound to say; and not to practise mental prayer.

It was at this time that my father was stricken by the illness of which he died. It lasted for some days. I went to look after him, more afflicted in soul than he in body. Distressed as I was, I forced myself into activity; and though in losing him I lost my greatest blessing and comfort, for he was always that to me, I was so determined not to let him see my grief for as long as he lived that I behaved as if I felt no grief at all. His chief ailment was a most acute pain in the back, which never left him. For three days he was practically unconscious; but, on the day of his death, the Lord restored his consciousness so completely that we were astonished, and he remained conscious until, half-way through the Creed, which he was repeating to himself, he died.

His confessor, who was a Dominican and a very learned man, used to say that he had not the least doubt he had gone straight to Heaven; he had been his confessor for some years and spoke highly of his purity of conscience. This Dominican father, who was a very good man and had a great fear of God, was of the very greatest help to me. I made my confessions to him and he took great pains to lead my soul aright and make me realize how near I was to perdition. He made me communicate once a fortnight; and gradually, as I got to know him, I began to tell him about my prayers. He told me never to leave these off, for they could not possibly do me anything but good. So I began to take them up once more and I never again abandoned them. My life became full of trials, because by means of prayer I learned more and more about my faults. On the one hand, God was calling me. On the other, I was following the world. All the things of God gave me great pleasure, yet I was tied and bound to those of the world. I suffered great trials in prayer, for the spirit was not master in me, but slave. I could not, therefore, shut myself up within myself (the procedure in which consisted my whole method of prayer) without at the same time shutting in a thousand vanities. Over a period of several years, I was more occupied in wishing my hour of prayer were over, and in listening whenever the clock struck, than in thinking of things that were good. Again and again I would rather have done any severe penance that might have been given me than practise recollection as a preliminary to prayer. I did not at once betake myself to prayer, and whenever I entered the oratory I used to feel so depressed that I had to summon up all my courage to make myself pray at all.

It is a great evil for a soul beset by so many dangers to be alone. I believe, if I had had anyone with whom to discuss all this, it would have helped me not to fall again. I would advise those who practise prayer, especially at first, to cultivate friendship with others of similar interests. This is a most important thing, if only because we can help each other by our prayers, and it is all the more so because it may bring us many other benefits. Since people can find comfort in the conversation and human sympathy of ordinary friendships, even when these are not altogether good, I do not know why anyone who is beginning to love and serve God in earnest should not be allowed to discuss his joys and trials with others—and people who practise prayer have plenty of both.

It is not without reason that I have dwelt upon this period of my life at such length. I spent nearly twenty years on that stormy sea, often falling in this way and each time rising again, but to little purpose, as I would only fall once more. So, more than eighteen of the twenty-eight years which have gone by since I began prayer have been spent in this battle and conflict. Now the reason why I have related all this is to make evident how, if a soul perseveres, the Lord, I am certain, will bring it to the harbour of salvation, just so, as far as can at present be told, He has brought me. I shall have a great deal to say about these consolations which the Lord gives to those who persevere in prayer.

The blessings possessed by one who practises prayer—I mean mental prayer—have been written of by many saints and good men. Glory be to God for this! If it were not so, I should not have assurance enough to dare to speak of it. I can say what I know by experience—namely, that no one who has begun this practice, however many sins he may commit, should ever forsake it. For it is the means by which we may amend our lives again, and without it amendment will be very much harder. So let him not be tempted to give it up. And anyone who has not begun to pray, I beg, for love of the Lord, not to miss so great a blessing. There is no place here for fear, but only desire. For, even if a person fails to make progress, or to

strive after perfection, yet he will gradually gain a knowledge of the road to Heaven. And if he perseveres, I hope
in the mercy of God, Whom no one has ever taken for a
Friend without being rewarded; and mental prayer, in my
view, is nothing but friendly intercourse, and frequent
solitary converse, with Him Who we know loves us.

However clearly I may wish to describe these matters
which concern prayer, they will be very obscure to anyone
who has no experience of it—for these matters concerning
prayer are difficult, and, if no director is available, very
hard to understand. Having gone through so much
myself, I am sorry for those who begin with books alone,
for it is extraordinary what a difference there is between
understanding a thing and knowing it by experience.

I want to describe this Prayer of Quiet to you, in the
way I have heard it talked about, and as the Lord has been
pleased to teach it to me, perhaps in order that I might
describe it to you. This is a supernatural state, and, however hard we try, we cannot reach it for ourselves; for it is
a state in which the soul enters into peace, or rather in
which the Lord gives it peace through His presence. In
this state all the faculties are stilled. The soul, in a way
which has nothing to do with the outward senses, realizes
that it is now very close to its God, and that, if it were but
a little closer, it would become one with Him through
union. This is not because it sees Him either with its
bodily or with its spiritual eyes. It is, as it were, in a
swoon, both inwardly and outwardly, so that the outward
man (let me call it the "body," and then you will understand me better) does not wish to move, but rests, like one
who has almost reached the end of his journey. The body
experiences the greatest delight and the soul is conscious
of a deep satisfaction. So glad is it merely to find itself near
the fountain that, even before it has begun to drink, it has
had its fill. There seems nothing left for it to desire. The
mind tries to occupy itself with only one thing, and the

memory has no desire to busy itself with more: they both see that this is the one thing needful and that anything else will unsettle them.

I think it will be well if I give some advice here to any of you whom the Lord, out of His goodness alone, has brought to this state. First of all, when such persons experience this joy, without knowing whence it has come to them, not knowing at least that they could not have achieved it of themselves, they are tempted to imagine that they can prolong it and they may even try not to breathe. This is ridiculous: we can no more control this prayer than we can make the day break, or stop night from falling; it is supernatural and something we cannot acquire. The most we can do to prolong this favour is to realize that we can neither diminish nor add to it, but, being most unworthy and undeserving of it can only receive it with thanksgiving.

Note carefully this piece of advice which I want to give you now. You will often find that these other two faculties [thought and memory] are of no help to you. It may come about that the soul is enjoying the highest degree of quiet, and that the understanding has soared so far aloft that what is happening to it seems not to be going on in its own house at all; it really seems to be a guest in somebody else's house, looking for other lodgings, since its own lodging no longer satisfies it and it cannot remain there for long together. Perhaps this is only my own experience and other people do not find it so. But, speaking for myself, I sometimes long to die because I cannot cure this wandering of the mind. At other times the mind seems to be settled in its own abode and to be remaining there with the will as its companion. When all three faculties work together it is wonderful. When the will finds itself in this state of quiet, it must take no more notice of the understanding than it would of a madman, for, if it tries to draw the understanding along with it, it is bound to grow preoccupied and restless, with the result that this state of prayer will be all effort and no gain and the soul will lose what God has been giving it without any effort of its own. When the understanding (or, to put it more clearly, the thought) wanders off after the most ridiculous things in the world, laugh at it and treat it as the silly thing it is. For thoughts will come and go, but the will is mistress and all-powerful, and will recall them without your having to trouble about it. But if you try to drag the understanding back by force, you lose your power over it. There is a saying that, if we try very hard to grasp all, we lose all; and so I think it is here. Experience will show you the truth of this.

Well, as I say, the soul is conscious of having reached this state of prayer, which is a quiet, deep and peaceful happiness of the will, without being able to decide precisely what it is, although it can clearly see how it differs from the happiness of the world. To have dominion over the whole world, with all its happiness, would not suffice to bring the soul such inward satisfaction as it enjoys now in the depths of its will. For other kinds of happiness in life, it seems to me, touch only the outward part of the will, which we might describe as its rind. Do you suppose it is of little importance that a soul which is often distracted should come to understand this truth and to find that, in order to speak to its Eternal Father and to take its delight in Him, it has no need to go to Heaven or to speak in a loud voice? However quietly we speak, He is so near that He will hear us: we need no wings to go in search of Him but have only to find a place where we can be alone and look upon Him present within us. Nor need we feel strange in the presence of so kind a Guest.

Those who are able to shut themselves up in this way within this little Heaven of the soul, wherein dwells the Maker of Heaven and earth, and who have formed the habit of looking at nothing and staying in no place which will distract these outward senses, may be sure that they are walking on an excellent road, and will come without fail to drink of the water of the fountain, for they will journey a long way in a short time. They are like one who travels in a ship, and, if he has a little good wind, reaches the end of his voyage in a few days.

It is a shame and unfortunate that through our own fault we don't understand ourselves or know who we are. Wouldn't it show great ignorance if someone when asked who he was didn't know, and didn't know his father or mother or from what country he came? Well now, if this would be so extremely stupid, we are incomparably more so when we do not strive to know who we are, but limit ourselves to considering only roughly these bodies. Because we have heard and because faith tells us so, we know we have souls. But we seldom consider the precious things that can be found in this soul, or who dwells within it, or its high value. Consequently, little effort is made to preserve its beauty. All our attention is taken up with the plainness of the diamond's setting or the outer wall of the castle; that is, with these bodies of ours.

Let us now come to the most intimate part of what the soul experiences. The persons who must speak of it are those who know it, for it cannot be understood, still less described. As I was about to write of this, I was wondering what it is the soul does during that time, when the Lord said these words to me: "It dies to itself wholly, daughter, in order that it may fix itself more and more upon Me; it is no longer itself that lives, but I. As it cannot comprehend what it understands, it is an understanding which understands not." The way in which this that we call union comes, and the nature of it, I do not know how to explain. It is described in mystical theology, but I am unable to use the proper terms, and I cannot understand what is meant by "mind" or how this differs from "soul" or "spirit." They all seem the same to me, though the soul sometimes issues from itself, like a fire that is burning and has become wholly flame.

I should like, with the help of God, to be able to describe the difference between union and rapture, or elevation, or what they call flight of the spirit, or transport—it is all one. I mean that these different names all refer to the same thing, which is also called ecstasy. I call it flight of the spirit—that, though substantially the same as other raptures, is interiorly experienced very differently. For sometimes suddenly a movement of the soul is felt that is so swift it seems the spirit is carried off, and at a fearful speed especially in the beginning. This is why strong courage is necessary for the one to whom God grants these favors, and even faith and confidence and a full surrender to our Lord so that He may do what He wants with the soul. It is such that the spirit truly seems to go forth from the body. On the other hand, it is clear that this person is not dead; at least, he cannot say whether for some moment he was in the body or not. It seems to him that he was entirely in another region different from this in which we live, where there is shown another light so different from earth's light that if he were to spend his whole life trying to imagine that light, along with the other things, he would be unable to do so. Within an instant so many things together are taught him. In the midst of these experiences that are both painful and delightful together, our Lord sometimes gives the soul feelings of jubilation and a strange prayer it doesn't understand. I am writing about this favor here so that if He grants it to you, you may give Him much praise and know what is taking place. It is, in my opinion, a deep union of the faculties; but our Lord nonetheless leaves them free that they might enjoy this joy—and the same goes for the senses—without understanding what it is they are enjoying or how they are enjoying. What I'm saying seems like gibberish, but certainly the experience takes place in this way, for the joy is so excessive the soul wouldn't want to enjoy it alone but wants to tell everyone about it so that they might help this soul praise our Lord. All its activity is directed to this praise. Oh, how many festivals and demonstrations the soul would organize, if it could, that all might know its joy! It seems it has found itself and that, like the father of the prodigal son, it would want to prepare a festival and invite all because it sees itself in an undoubtedly safe place, at least for the time being.

To be silent and conceal this great impulse of happiness, when experiencing it, is no small pain. Saint Francis must have felt this impulse when the robbers struck him, for he ran through the fields crying out and telling them that he was the herald of the great King; and also other saints must feel it who go to deserts to be able to proclaim as Saint Francis these praises of their God. I knew a saint named Friar Peter of Alcantara—for I believe from the way he lived that he was one—who did this very thing, and those who at one time listened to him thought he was crazy. Oh, what blessed madness! The soul goes about like a person who has drunk a great deal but not so much as to be drawn out of his senses; or like a person suffering melancholy who has not lost his reason completely but cannot free himself from what is in his imagination—nor can anyone else. These are inelegant comparisons for something so precious, but I can't think up any others. The joy makes a person so forgetful of self that he doesn't advert to, nor can he speak of anything other than, the praises of God that proceed from his joy.

I used sometimes to experience in an elementary form, and very fleetingly, what I shall now describe. When picturing Christ, and sometimes even when reading, I used unexpectedly to experience a consciousness of the presence of God, of such a kind that I could not possibly doubt that He was within me or that I was wholly engulfed in Him. The soul is suspended in such a way that it seems to be completely outside itself. The will loves; the memory, I think, is almost lost; while the understanding, I believe, though it is not lost, does not reason. One year, on Saint Paul's Day, when I was at Mass, I saw a complete representation of this most sacred Humanity, just as in a picture of His resurrection body, in very great beauty and majesty. I saw it only with the eyes of the soul. At certain times it really seemed to me that it was an image I was seeing; but on many other occasions I thought it was no image, but Christ Himself, such was the brightness with which He was pleased to reveal Himself to me. If I were to spend years and years imagining how to invent anything so beautiful, I could not do it, and I do not even know how I should try, for, even in its whiteness and radiance alone, it exceeds all that we can imagine. It is not a radiance which dazzles, but a soft whiteness and an infused radiance which, without wearying the eyes, causes them the greatest delight; nor are they wearied by the brightness which they see in seeing this Divine beauty. So different from any earthly light is the brightness and light now revealed to the eyes that, by comparison with it, the brightness of our sun seems quite dim and we should never want to open our eyes again for the purpose of seeing it. It is as if we were to look at a very clear stream, in a bed of crystal, reflecting the sun's rays. Not that the sun, or any other such light, enters into the vision: on the contrary, it is like a natural light and all other kinds of light seem artificial. It is a light which never gives place to night, and, being always light, is disturbed by nothing. It is of such a kind, indeed, that no one, however powerful his intellect, could, in the whole course of his life, imagine it as it is. And so quickly does God reveal it to us that, even if we needed to open our eyes in order to see it, there would not be time for us to do so. But it is all the same whether they are open or closed: if the Lord is pleased for us to see it, we shall do so even against our will. There is nothing powerful enough to divert our attention from it, and we can neither resist it nor attain to it by any diligence or care of our own. This I have conclusively proved by experience.

9

THE MASTER SHOEMAKER

Jn diefem Lichte hat mein Geift alsbald durch alles gefeben, und an allen Creaturen, fo mol an Kraut und Gras GOtt ertant, wer der fen, und mas fein Wille fen: auch fo ift alsbald in diefem Lichte mein Willen gemach: fen mit groffem Trieh, das Wefen GOttes zu befchreiben.

In this light my spirit suddenly saw through all, and in and by all, the creatures; even in herbs and grass it knew God, who he is and how he is and what his will is. And suddenly in that light my will was set on by a mighty impulse to describe the Being of God.

———Jacob Boehme
Aurora

The passages within this chapter are from the following sources:

The Confessions of Jacob Boehme, compiled and edited by W. Scott Palmer (New York: Harper-Collins, 1954), chapters 1–3, 6.

Dialogues on the Supersensual Life, translated by William Law and others, edited by Bernard Holland (New York: Frederick Ungar Publishing Co.), pp. 13–16.

◆　◆　◆

Jacob Boehme (1575–1624) was born into a poor peasant family near the city of Gorlitz in eastern Germany. During Boehme's time, Gorlitz was a prosperous trade center with an advanced non-feudal society. The great religious reformer Martin Luther had died just thirty years previously and the church in Gorlitz was staunchly Lutheran.

As a boy, Jacob watched the herds in the fields and received no more than the most elementary education. At 14, not having the strength and health for farm work, he was apprenticed to the village shoemaker to learn the trade of cobbling. But soon, Jacob's pensiveness and diligent study of the scriptures became an annoyance to the master, and he was dismissed. For several years he was forced to earn his way as a traveling shoemaker, still absorbed in religious study.

In 1595, Jacob returned to Gorlitz and became a master shoemaker in his own right. A statute of the shoemaker's guild of 1573 states: "When a journeyman becomes a master, he shall marry within half a year." Boehme evidently complied with this dictate, for he soon married the daughter of a Gorlitz butcher and began a family which would eventually include four children. With his wife's substantial dowry he set up his own shop and became a prominent citizen. His high standing, however, did not last.

In the spring of 1600, then 25 years old, Boehme underwent a profound mystical experience. He spoke of his experience to no one for several years, but continued to catch occasional glimpses and fragments of this extraordinary and unexpected consciousness. After ten years, another sudden illumination brought a coherence and stability to his understanding and he felt a "firelike" impulse to write, not for publication, but as a "memorial" for himself. His first book was written in the early morning hours before work and was entitled *Aurora* (or "Dawn Glow").

Although he had no intention of publishing the work, he did show it to an old friend. This friend was Carl von Ender, a widely traveled and educated nobleman. Von Ender, without Boehme's knowledge or consent, had copies of the manuscript made and circulated among his aristocratic friends. A copy fell into the hands of Gregorius Richter, chief pastor in Gorlitz. From the pulpit, Richter denounced Boehme as a dangerous heretic and demanded his arrest.

Boehme was soon summoned before the City Magistrates and forbidden to write further, under threat of exile. The mystic shoemaker became a mistrusted curiosity to his neighbors. However, he did continue to find support among the nobility of the country.

For five years Boehme obeyed the injunction against writing, but with difficulty. Eventually, after deliberating over Jesus's parable of the ten talents, he again took pen in hand. During the next five years (until his death in 1624 at age 49), Boehme produced thirty books. One of these, *The Way To Christ*, drew fresh attacks from Gregorious Richter:

> There are as many blasphemies in this shoemaker's book as there are lines; it smells of shoemaker's pitch and filthy blacking.

Boehme was now forced into exile, but was supported by his growing coterie of friends and admirers who had continued to circulate his works in secret. In time he fell ill and was returned to his home town and died in his home in Gorlitz.

Boehme's vast writings are considered difficult, sometimes incomprehensible, due in part to his uneducated use of language and his unique mystical symbolism. As mentioned, the shoemaker's early works were not meant for publication. His later books improve in clarity and reflect the influence of his aristocratic mentors.

Throughout his books, Boehme makes infrequent, incidental references to his own life and experiences. These autobiographical passages are widely scattered and were not collected and arranged in one volume until this century, by W. Scott Palmer. From Palmer's book, *The Confessions of Jacob Boehme*, we hear Boehme speak candidly of his own experiences.

♦   ♦   ♦

O that I had but the pen of a man, and were able therewith to write down the spirit of knowledge! I can but stammer of great mysteries like a child that is beginning to speak; so very little can the earthly tongue express of that which the spirit comprehends. Yet I will venture to try whether I may incline some to seek the pearl of true knowledge, and myself labour in the works of God in my paradisical garden of roses; for the longing of the eternal nature-mother drives me on to write and to exercise myself in this my knowledge.

Art has not wrote this, neither was there any time to consider how to set it punctually down, according to the right understanding of letters, but all was ordered according to the direction of the Spirit, which often went in haste; so that in many words letters may be wanting, and in some places a capital letter for a word. The Penman's hand, by reason he was not accustomed to it, did often shake; and though I could have written in a more accurate, fair, and plain manner, yet the reason I did not was this, that the burning fire often forced forward with speed, and the hand and pen must hasten directly after it; for that fire comes and goes as a sudden shower. I can write nothing of myself but as a child which neither knows nor understands anything, which neither has ever been learnt; and I write only that which the Lord vouchsafes to know in me according to the measure as himself manifests in me.

I never desired to know anything of the Divine Mystery, much less understood I the way to seek and find it. I knew nothing of it, which is the condition of poor laymen in their simplicity.

I sought only after the heart of Jesus Christ, that I might hide myself therein from the wrathful anger of God and the violent assaults of the Devil. And I besought the Lord earnestly for his Holy Spirit and his grace, that he would please to bless and guide me in him, and take that away from me which turned me from him. I resigned myself wholly to him, that I might not live to my own will, but his; and that he only might lead and direct me, to the end I might be his child in his son Jesus.

In this my earnest and Christian seeking and desire (wherein I suffered many a shrewd repulse, but at last resolved rather to put myself in hazard than leave off), the Gate was opened to me, that in one quarter of an hour I saw and knew more than if I had been many years together at an University, at which I exceedingly admired and thereupon turned my praise to God for it.

So that I did not only greatly wonder at it, but did also exceedingly rejoice; and presently it came powerfully into my mind to set the same down in writing, for a memorial for myself, though I could very hardly apprehend the same in my external man and express it with the pen. Yet, however, I must begin to labour in this great mystery as a child that goes to school.

I saw it as in a great deep in the internal; for I had a thorough view of the Universe, as a complex moving fulness wherein all things are couched and wrapped up; but it was impossible for me to explain the same.

Yet it opened itself in me, from time to time, as in a young plant. It was with me for the space of twelve years, and was as it were breeding. I found a powerful instigation within me before I could bring it forth into external form of writing; but whatever I could apprehend with the external principle of my mind, that I wrote down.

Afterwards, however, the Sun shone upon me a good while, but not constantly, for sometimes the Sun hid itself, and then I knew not nor well understood my own labour. Man must confess that his knowledge is not his own but from God, who manifests the Ideas of Wisdom to the soul, in what measure he pleases.

It is not to be understood that my reason is greater or higher than that of all other men living; but I am the Lord's twig or branch, and a very mean and little spark of his light; he may set me where he pleases, I cannot hinder him in that.

Neither is this my natural will, that I can do it by my own small ability; for if the Spirit were withdrawn from me, then I could neither know nor understand my own writings.

O gracious amiable Blessedness and great Love, how sweet art thou! How friendly and courteous art thou! How pleasant and lovely is thy relish and taste! How ravishing sweetly dost thou smell! O noble Light, and bright Glory, who can apprehend thy exceeding beauty? How comely adorned is thy love! How curious and excellent are thy colours! And all this eternally. Who can express it?

Or why and what do I write, whose tongue does but stammer like a child which is learning to speak? With what shall I compare it? or to what shall I liken it? Shall I compare it with the love of this world? No, that is but a mere dark valley to it.

O immense Greatness! I cannot compare thee with any thing, but only with the resurrection from the dead; there will the Love-Fire rise up again in us, and rekindle again our astringent, bitter, and cold, dark and dead powers, and embrace us most courteously and friendly.

O gracious, amiable, blessed Love and clear bright Light, tarry with us, I pray thee, for the evening is at hand.

I am a sinful and mortal man, as well as thou, and I must every day and hour grapple, struggle, and fight with the Devil.

But when he is overcome, then the heavenly gate opens in my spirit, and then the spirit sees the divine and heavenly Being, not externally beyond the body, but in the well-spring of the heart. There rises up a flash of the Light in the sensibility or thoughts of the brain, and therein the Spirit does contemplate.

When the flash is caught in the fountain of the heart, then the Holy Spirit rises up, in the seven unfolding fountain spirits, into the brain, like the dawning of the day, the morning redness.[1] In that Light the one sees the other, feels the other, smells the other, tastes the other, and hears the other, and is as if the whole Deity rose up therein.

Herein the spirit sees into the depth of the Deity; for in God near and far off is all one; and that same God is in his three-foldness as well in the body of a holy soul as in heaven.

From this God I take my knowledge and from no other thing; neither will I know any other thing than that same God. And he it is which makes that assurance in my spirit, that I steadfastly believe and trust in him.

Though an angel from heaven should tell this to me, yet for all that I could not believe it, much less lay hold on it; for I should always doubt whether it was certainly so or no. But the Sun itself arises in my spirit, and therefore I am most sure of it.

I marvel that God should reveal himself thus fully to such a simple man, and that he thus impels him also to set

---

[1]Boehme certainly had no knowledge of the Hindu concept of Kundalini and the seven chakras, yet this description of a spiritual power rising to the brain through seven unfolding fountains is remarkably similar.

it down in writing; whereas there are many learned writers which could set it forth and express it better, and demonstrate it more exactly and fully than I, that am a scorn and fool to the world.

But I neither can nor will oppose him; for I often stood in great striving against him, that if it was not his impulse and will he would be pleased to take it from me; but I find that with my striving against him I have merely gathered stones for this building.

Now I am climbed up and mounted so very high that I dare not look back for fear a giddiness should take me; and I have now but a short length of ladder to the mark to which it is the whole desire, longing, and delight of my heart to reach fully.

Men have always been of the opinion that heaven is many hundred, nay, many thousand, miles distant from the face of the earth, and that God dwells only in that heaven.

Some have undertaken to measure this height and distance, and have produced many strange and monstrous devices. Indeed, before my knowledge and revelation of God, I held that only to be the true heaven which, in a round circumference, very azure of a light blue colour, extends itself above the stars; supposing that God had therein his peculiar Being, and did rule only in the power of his Holy Spirit in this world.

But when this had given me many a hard blow and repulse, doubtless from the Spirit, which had a great longing yearning towards me at last I fell into a very deep melancholy and heavy sadness, when I beheld and contemplated the great Deep of this world, also the sun and stars, the clouds, rain and snow, and considered in my spirit the whole creation of the world.

Wherein then I found, in all things, evil and good, love and anger; in the inanimate creatures, in wood, stones, earth and the elements, as also in men and beasts.

Moreover I considered the little spark of light, man, what he should be esteemed for with God, in comparison of this great work and fabric of heaven and earth.

And finding that in all things there was evil and good, as well in the elements as in the creatures, and that it went as well in this world with the wicked as with the virtuous, honest and godly; also that the barbarous people had the best countries in their possession, and that they had more prosperity in their ways than the virtuous, honest and godly had; I was thereupon very melancholy, perplexed and exceedingly troubled, no Scripture could comfort or satisfy me though I was very well acquainted with it and versed therein; at which time the Devil would by no means stand idle, but was often beating into me many heathenish thoughts which I will here be silent in.

Yet when in this affliction and trouble I elevated my spirit (which then I understood very little or nothing at all what it was), I earnestly raised it up into God, as with a great storm or onset, wrapping up my whole heart and mind, as also all my thoughts and whole will and resolution, incessantly to wrestle with the Love and Mercy of God, and not to give over unless he blessed me, that is, unless he enlightened me with his Holy Spirit, whereby I might understand his will and be rid of my sadness. And then the Spirit did break through.

But when in my resolved zeal I gave so hard an assault, storm, and onset upon God and upon all the gates of hell, as if I had more reserves of virtue and power ready, with a resolution to hazard my life upon it (which assuredly were not in my ability without the assistance of the Spirit of God), suddenly my spirit did break through the gates of hell, even into the innermost moving of the Deity, and there I was embraced in love as a bridegroom embraces his dearly beloved bride.

The greatness of the triumphing that was in my spirit I cannot express either in speaking or writing; neither can it be compared to any thing but that wherein life is generated in the midst of death. It is like the resurrection from the dead.

In this light my spirit suddenly saw through all, and in and by all, the creatures; even in herbs and grass it knew God, who he is and how he is and what his will is. And suddenly in that light my will was set on by a mighty impulse to describe the Being of God.

But because I could not presently apprehend the deepest movings of God and comprehend them in my reason, there passed almost twelve years before the exact understanding thereof was given me.

And it was with me as with a young tree, which is planted in the ground and at first is young and tender, and flourishing to the eye, especially if it comes on lustily in its growing; but does not bear fruit presently, and though it has blossoms they fall off: also frost and snow and many a cold wind beat upon it before it comes to any growth and bearing of fruit.

So also it went with my spirit: the first fire was but a beginning and not a constant and lasting light; since that time many a cold wind blew upon it, yet never extinguished it.

The tree was also often tempted to try whether it could bear fruit, and showed itself with blossoms; but the blossoms were struck off till this very time, wherein it stands in its fruit.

From this light now it is that I have my knowledge, as also my will, impulse and driving.

I have neither pen that can write nor words that can express what the exceeding sweet grace of God in Christ is. I myself have found it by experience in this my way and course, and therefore certainly know that I have a sure ground from which I write. And I would from the bottom of my heart most willingly impart the same to my brethren in the love of Christ, who, if they will follow my faithful

childlike counsels, will find by experience in themselves
from whence it is that my simple mind knows and understands great mysteries.

Leaving the Confessions, we turn to one of Boehme's last
major books, written two years before his death, entitled
Dialogues on the Supersensual Life. This book is written in
the form of a dialogue between a novice disciple and an
enlightened master. Here the master offers the student
some practical advice on attaining the inner experience.
From Dialogues I and II:

Disciple
Sir, how may I come to the Supersensual Life, so that I
may see God, and may hear God speak?

Master
Son, when thou canst throw thyself into THAT, where no
Creature dwelleth, though it be but for a moment, then
thou hearest what God speaketh.

Disciple
Is that where no Creature dwelleth near at hand, or is it
afar off?

Master
It is *in thee*. And if thou canst, my Son, for a while but
cease from all thy thinking and willing, then thou shalt
hear the unspeakable words of God.

Disciple
How can I hear him speak, when I stand still from thinking and willing?

Master
When thou standest still from the thinking of Self, and the

willing of Self. When both thy intellect and will are quiet, and passive to the expressions of the Eternal Word and Spirit; and when thy soul is winged up and above that which is temporal, the outward senses and the imagination being locked up by holy abstraction, then the Eternal Hearing, Seeing and Speaking will be revealed in thee, and so God heareth and seeth through thee, being now the organ of *his* Spirit, and so God speaketh in *thee*, and whispereth to thy Spirit, and thy Spirit heareth his voice.

Disciple

But being I am in Nature, and thus bound as with my own chains, and by my own natural will, pray be so kind, Sir, as to tell me, how I may come *through* Nature into the Supersensual and Supernatural Ground, without the destroying of Nature?

Master

It is even so as thou hast said. All is confusion if thou hast no more than the dim Light of Nature, or unsanctified and unregenerated Reason to guide thee by, and if only the Eye of Time be opened in thee, which cannot pierce beyond its own limit. Wherefore seek the Fountain of Light, waiting in the deep ground of thy soul for the rising there of the Sun of Righteousness, whereby the Light of Nature in thee, with the properties thereof, will be made to shine seven times brighter than ordinary. For it shall receive the stamp, image and impression of the Supersensual and Supernatural, so that the sensual and rational life will hence be brought into the most perfect order and harmony.

Disciple

But how am I to wait for the rising of this glorious Sun, and how am I to seek in the Centre this Fountain of Light, which may enlighten me throughout and bring my properties into perfect harmony?

Master

Cease but from thine own activity, steadfastly fixing thine Eye upon *one Point*, and with a strong purpose relying upon the promised Grace of God in Christ, to bring thee out of thy Darkness into his marvellous Light. For this end gather in all thy thoughts, and by faith press into the Centre, laying hold upon the Word of God, which is infallible, and which hath called thee. Be thou then obedient to his call, and be silent before the Lord, sitting alone with him in thy inmost and most hidden cell, thy mind being centrally united in itself, and attending his Will in the patience of hope. So shall thy Light break forth as the Morning, and after the redness thereof is passed, the Sun himself which thou waitest for, shall arise unto thee, and under his most healing wings thou shalt greatly rejoice; ascending and descending in his bright and salutiferous beams. Behold this is the true Supersensual Ground of Life.

10

THE JOURNAL OF GEORGE FOX

I saw into that which was without end, things which cannot be uttered, and of the greatness and infinitude of the love of God, which cannot be expressed by words. . . . This I saw in the pure openings of the Light without the help of any man.

————George Fox
The Journal

♦ ♦ ♦

George Fox (1624–1691) was born in England the year of
Jacob Boehme's death. Boehme's works were being translated and published in England at the time Fox began his
missionary labors, and many of Fox's followers were
familiar with Boehme's writings. Many parallels in the
experiences of these two men will be evident. For
instance, Fox shared Boehme's mystical knowledge of the
nature of herbs, so much so that he briefly considered
becoming a physician.

But it was not as a physician that George Fox became
known throughout England and the new world, America;
but as the founder of a new and "radical" religion, Quakerism. It had not been Fox's intention to begin a new sect
separate from the existing church. But the circumstances
of his life led to this remarkable event. By the time of his
death, Quakerism was firmly established and had
achieved a degree of official recognition by the government. At his death, there were 50,000 Friends (also called
Quakers), with well-organized meetings in Great Britain,
Ireland, Holland, New York, Pennsylvania, Virginia, and
other states.

Fox's ministry began as a solitary voice whose message inspired men to either devotion or actual rage. He
was described as a man of unusual charisma. The uncanny
power of his eyes was often noted and even admitted to
by his detractors. William Penn, the founder of Pennsylvania, described Fox as follows.

> The inwardness and weight of his spirit, the rever-
> ence and solemnity of his address and behaviour,
> and the fewness and fullness of his words have
> often struck even strangers with admiration, as
> they used to reach others with consolation. The
> most awful, living, reverent frame I ever felt or

beheld, I must say, was his in prayer. And truly it
was a testimony that he knew and lived nearer to
the Lord than other men; for they that know him
most will see most reason to approach him with
reverence and fear.

He was of an innocent life, no busybody, nor self-
seeker, neither touchy nor critical; what fell upon
him was very inoffensive, if not very edifying. So
meek, contented, modest, easy, steady, tender, it
was a pleasure to be in his company. He exercised
no authority but over evil, and that everywhere
and in all, but with love, compassion, and long-
suffering, a most merciful man, as ready to forgive
as unapt to take or give an offence. Thousands can
truly say he was of an excellent spirit and savour
among them, and because thereof, the most excellent spirits loved him with an unfeigned and
unfading love.

He was an incessant labourer, for in his younger
time, before his many great and deep sufferings
and travels had enfeebled his body for itinerant
services, he laboured much in the word, and doctrine and discipline, in England, Scotland and Ireland, turning many to God, and confirming those
that were convinced of the Truth, and settling
good order as to church affairs among them.

I write by knowledge and not report; and my witness is true, having been with him for weeks and
months together on divers occasions, and those of
the nearest and most exercising nature, and that
by night and by day, by sea and by land, in this
and in foreign countries; and I can say I never saw
him out of his place, or not a match for every
service or occasion.

In the British churches of Fox's day, it was permissible at the end of a service for any male member of the congregation to pose a question or to give some message of his own. Fox took advantage of this custom as he traveled from church to church. He would speak of the transforming power of the inner Christ, of which he claimed to have had first-hand experience just as the apostles of old. He spoke everywhere of the "Light which lighteth every man," that Light being the only true authority. In numerous instances, the effect of Fox's message was disasterous—he would be physically ousted from the church and beaten. He was frequently imprisoned. Yet always, there were others among the parishioners who felt wonderfully moved by Fox's message and the ranks of the Society of Friends quickly grew. This rapid development occurred despite the fact that becoming a Quaker often meant subjecting oneself to harsh persecution. Thousands of Quakers were imprisoned and their properties seized. Between 1661 and 1697, 338 Quakers died while in prison. Often such punishment was handed down for an offense no greater than the Quaker's refusal to take an oath. Such persecutions continued until the revolution of 1688. New laws under William and Mary brought general relief to the Quakers.

In 1652 Fox met Margaret Fell, his future wife. She attended several of Fox's meetings and was struck by a question he often posed: "You will say, Christ saith this and the Apostles say this, but what canst *thou* say? Art *thou* a child of Light and hast thou walked in the Light, and what thou speakest, is it inwardly from God?" She was instrumental in providing shelter and support for those under persecution and in providing funds for the travels of Fox and others.

In 1671–1673, Fox visited North America, organizing the Quaker communities in existence there. Many Quakers had immigrated to the New World to escape the persecutions at home.

In 1675, Fox dictated his memoires, which were published after his death as *The Journal of George Fox*. The Journal remains a significant book to the 200,000 Quakers of today. These excerpts are from the first two chapters of the Journal, when Fox describes his early life and his first transformation into the consciousness of inner light.

◆　◆　◆

That all may know the dealings of the Lord with me, and the various exercises, trials, and troubles through which He led me, in order to prepare and fit me for the work unto which He had appointed me, and may thereby be drawn to admire and glorify His infinite wisdom and goodness, I think fit (before I proceed to set forth my public travels in the service of Truth) briefly to mention how it was with me in my youth, and how the work of the Lord was begun, and gradually carried on in me, even from my childhood.

I was born in the month called July, 1624, at Drayton-in-the-Clay, in Leicestershire. My father's name was Christopher Fox; he was by profession a weaver, an honest man; and there was a Seed of God in him. The neighbours called him Righteous Christer. My mother was an upright woman; her maiden name was Mary Lago, of the family of the Lagos, and of the stock of the martyrs.

In my very young years I had a gravity and stayedness of mind and spirit not usual in children; insomuch that when I saw old men behave lightly and wantonly towards each other, I had a dislike thereof raised in my heart, and said within myself, "If ever I come to be a man, surely I shall not do so, nor be so wanton."

When I came towards nineteen years of age, being upon business at a fair, one of my cousins, whose name was Bradford, having another professor[1] with him, came and asked me to drink part of a jug of beer with them. I, being thirsty, went in with them, for I loved any who had a sense of good, or that sought after the Lord.

When we had drunk a glass apiece, they began to drink healths, and called for more drink, agreeing together that he that would not drink should pay all. I was grieved that any who made profession of religion should offer to do so. They grieved me very much, having never had such a thing put to me before by any sort of people. Wherefore I rose up, and, putting my hand in my pocket, took out a groat, and laid it upon the table before them, saying, "If it be so, I will leave you."

So I went away; and when I had done my business returned home; but did not go to bed that night, nor could I sleep, but sometimes walked up and down, and sometimes prayed and cried to the Lord, who said unto me: "Thou seest how young people go together into vanity, and old people into the earth; thou must forsake all, young and old, keep out of all, and be as a stranger unto all."

Then, at the command of God, the ninth of the Seventh month, 1643, I left my relations, and broke off all familiarity or fellowship with young or old. I passed to Lutterworth, where I stayed some time. From thence I went to Northampton, where also I made some stay; then passed to Newport-Pagnel, whence, after I had stayed awhile, I went to Barnet, in the Fourth month, called June,[2] in the year 1644.

---

[1]*Professor* here means a Christian who merely professes his faith. (Note is from original text of *The Journal of George Fox*, edited by Rufus M. Jones [Richmond, IN: Friends United Press, 1976].)

[2]Until 1752, the English year began in March, so that by the calendar then in use, June was the fourth month. (Note is from original text of *The Journal of George Fox*, edited by Rufus M. Jones [Richmond, IN: Friends United Press, 1976].)

As I thus traveled through the country, professors took notice of me, and sought to be acquainted with me; but I was afraid of them, for I was sensible they did not possess what they professed.

During the time I was at Barnet a strong temptation to despair came upon me. I then saw how Christ was tempted, and mighty troubles I was in. Sometimes I kept myself retired to my chamber, and often walked solitary in the Chase to wait upon the Lord. I wondered why these things should come to me. I looked upon myself, and said, "Was I ever so before?" Then I thought, because I had forsaken my relations I had done amiss against them.

I was about twenty years of age when these exercises came upon me; and some years I continued in that condition, in great trouble; and fain I would have put it from me. I went to many a priest to look for comfort, but found no comfort from them.

From Barnet I went to London, where I took a lodging, and was under great misery and trouble there; for I looked upon the great professors of the city of London, and saw all was dark and under the chain of darkness. I had an uncle there, one Pickering, a Baptist; the Baptists were tender[3] then; yet I could not impart my mind to him, nor join with them; for I saw all, young and old, where they were. Some tender people would have had me stay, but I was fearful, and returned homeward into Leicestershire, having a regard upon my mind to my parents and relations, lest I should grieve them, for I understood they were troubled at my absence.

Being returned into Leicestershire, my relations would have had me married; but I told them I was but a lad, and must get wisdom. Others would have had me join the

[3]*Tender* is one of George Fox's favorite words. The persons to whom it is applied are religiously inclined, serious, and earnest in their search for spiritual realities. (Note is from original text of *The Journal of George Fox*, edited by Rufus M. Jones.)

auxiliary band among the soldiery, but I refused, and was grieved that they offered such things to me, being a tender youth. Then I went to Coventry, where I took a chamber for awhile at a professor's house, till people began to be acquainted with me, for there were many tender people in that town. After some time I went into my own country again, and continued about a year, in great sorrow and trouble, and walked many nights by myself.

After this I went to another ancient priest at Mancetter, in Warwickshire, and reasoned with him about the ground of despair and temptations. But he was ignorant of my condition; he bade me take tobacco and sing psalms. Tobacco was a thing I did not love, and psalms I was not in a state to sing; I could not sing. He bade me come again, and he would tell me many things; but when I came he was angry and pettish, for my former words had displeased him. He told my troubles, sorrows, and griefs to his servants, so that it got out among the milk-lasses. It grieved me that I should have opened my mind to such a one. I saw they were all miserable comforters, and this increased my troubles upon me. I heard of a priest living about Tamworth, who was accounted an experienced man. I went seven miles to him, but found him like an empty, hollow cask.

After this I went to another, one Macham, a priest in high account. He would needs give me some physic, and I was to have been let blood; but they could not get one drop of blood from me, either in arms or head (though they endeavoured to do so), my body being, as it were, dried up with sorrows, grief and troubles, which were so great upon me that I could have wished I had never been born, or that I had been born blind, that I might never have seen wickedness or vanity; and deaf, that I might never have heard vain and wicked words, or the Lord's name blasphemed.

At another time, as I was walking in a field on a First-day morning, the Lord opened unto me that being bred at Oxford or Cambridge was not enough to fit and qualify men to be ministers of Christ; and I wondered at it, because it was the common belief of people. But I saw it clearly as the Lord opened it unto me, and was satisfied, and admired the goodness of the Lord, who had opened this thing unto me that morning. This struck at priest Stephen's ministry, namely, that "to be bred at Oxford or Cambridge was not enough to make a man fit to be a minister of Christ." So that which opened in me I saw struck at the priest's ministry.

But my relations were much troubled that I would not go with them to hear the priest; for I would go into the orchard or the fields, with my Bible, by myself. I asked them, "Did not the Apostle say to believers that they needed no man to teach them, but as the anointing tea-cheth them?" Though they knew this was Scripture, and that it was true, yet they were grieved because I could not be subject in this matter, to go to hear the priest with them. I saw that to be a true believer was another thing than they looked upon it to be; and I saw that being bred at Oxford or Cambridge did not qualify or fit a man to be a minister of Christ; what then should I follow such for! So neither them, nor any of the dissenting people, could I join with; but was as a stranger to all, relying wholly upon the Lord Jesus Christ.

At another time it was opened in me that God, who made the world, did not dwell in temples made with hands. This at first seemed a strange word, because both priests and people used to call their temples, or churches, dreadful places, holy ground, and the temples of God. But the Lord showed me clearly that He did not dwell in these temples which men had commanded and set up, but in people's hearts; for both Stephen and the apostle Paul bore testimony that He did not dwell in temples made

with hands, not even in that which He had once commanded to be built, since He put an end to it; but that His
people were His temple, and He dwelt in them.

This opened in me as I walked in the fields to my
relations' house. When I came there they told me that
Nathaniel Stephens, the priest, had been there, and told
them he was afraid of me, for going after new lights. I
smiled in myself, knowing what the Lord had opened in
me concerning him and his brethren; but I told not my
relations, who, though they saw beyond the priests, yet
went to hear them, and were grieved because I would not
go also. But I brought them Scriptures, and told them
there was an anointing within man to teach him, and that
the Lord would teach His people Himself.

Now, though I had great openings, yet great trouble
and temptation came many times upon me; so that when
it was day I wished for night, and when it was night I
wished for day; and by reason of the openings I had in my
troubles, I could say as David said, "Day unto day uttereth
speech, and night unto night showeth knowledge." When
I had openings they answered one another and answered
the Scriptures; for I had great openings of the Scriptures:
and when I was in troubles, one trouble also answered to
another.

About the beginning of the year 1647 I was moved of
the Lord to go into Derbyshire, where I met with some
friendly people, and had many discourses with them.
Then, passing into the Peak country, I met with more
friendly people, and with some in empty high notions.
Travelling through some parts of Leicestershire, and into
Nottinghamshire, I met with a tender people, and a very
tender woman, whose name was Elizabeth Hooton. With
these I had some meetings and discourses; but my troubles continued, and I was often under great temptations.

I fasted much, walked abroad in solitary places many
days, and often took my Bible, and sat in hollow trees and

lonesome places till night came on; and frequently in the night walked mournfully about by myself; for I was a man of sorrows in the time of the first workings of the Lord in me.

During all this time I was never joined in profession of religion with any, but gave up myself to the Lord, having forsaken all evil company, taken leave of father and mother, and all other relations, and travelled up and down as a stranger in the earth, which way the Lord inclined my heart; taking a chamber to myself in the town where I came, and tarrying, sometimes more, sometimes less, in a place. For I durst not stay long in a place, being afraid both of professor and profane, lest, being a tender young man, I should be hurt by conversing much with either. For this reason I kept much as a stranger, seeking heavenly wisdom and getting knowledge from the Lord, and was brought off from outward things to rely on the Lord alone.

Though my exercises and troubles were very great, yet were they not so continual but that I had some intermissions, and I was sometimes brought into such an heavenly joy that I thought I had been in Abraham's bosom.

Now, after I had received that opening from the Lord, that to be bred at Oxford or Cambridge was not sufficient to fit a man to be a minister of Christ, I regarded the priests less, and looked more after the Dissenting people. Among them I saw there was some tenderness; and many of them came afterwards to be convinced, for they had some openings.

But as I had forsaken the priests, so I left the separate preachers also, and those esteemed the most experienced people; for I saw there was none among them all that could speak to my condition. When all my hopes in them and in all men were gone, so that I had nothing outwardly to help me, nor could I tell what to do, then, oh, then, I heard a voice which said, "There is one, even Christ Jesus, that can speak to they condition"; and when I heard it, my heart did leap for joy.

Then the Lord let me see why there was none upon the earth that could speak to my condition, namely, that I might give Him all the glory. For all are concluded under sin, and shut up in unbelief, as I had been; that Jesus Christ might have the pre-eminence, who enlightens, and gives grace, and faith, and power. Thus when God doth work, who shall hinder it? and *this I knew experimentally*.

My desire after the Lord grew stronger, and zeal in the pure knowledge of God, and of Christ alone, without the help of any man, book, or writing. For though I read the Scriptures that spoke of Christ and of God, yet I knew Him not, but by revelation, as He who hath the key did open, and as the Father of Life drew me to His Son by His Spirit. Then the Lord gently led me along, and let me see His love, which was endless and eternal, surpassing all the knowledge that men have in the natural state, or can obtain from history or books; and that love let me see myself, as I was without Him.

When I myself was in the deep, shut up under all, I could not believe that I should ever overcome; my troubles, my sorrows, and my temptations were so great that I thought many times I should have despaired, I was so tempted. But when Christ opened to me how He was tempted by the same devil, and overcame him and bruised his head, and that through Him and His power, light, grace, and Spirit, I should overcome also, I had confidence in Him; so He it was that opened to me when I was shut up and had no hope nor faith. Christ, who had enlightened me, gave me His light to believe in; He gave me hope, which He Himself revealed in me, and He gave me His Spirit and grace, which I found sufficient in the deeps and in weakness.

Thus, in the deepest miseries, and in the greatest sorrows and temptations, that many times beset me, the Lord in His mercy did keep me.

I found that there were two thirsts in me—the one after the creatures, to get help and strength there, and the other after the Lord, the Creator, and His Son Jesus Christ. I saw all the world could do me no good; if I had had a king's diet, palace, and attendance, all would have been as nothing; for nothing gave me comfort but the Lord by His power. At another time I saw the great love of God, and was filled with admiration at the infiniteness of it.

One day, when I had been walking solitarily abroad, and was come home, I was taken up in the love of God, so that I could not but admire the greatness of His love; and while I was in that condition, it was opened unto me by the eternal light and power, and I therein clearly saw that all was done and to be done in and by Christ, and how He conquers and destroys this tempter the devil, and all his works, and is atop of him; and that all these troubles were good for me, and temptations for the trial of my faith, which Christ had given me.

The Lord opened me, that I saw all through these troubles and temptations. My living faith was raised, that I saw all was done by Christ the life, and my belief was in Him.

When at any time my condition was veiled, my secret belief was stayed firm, and hope underneath held me, as an anchor in the bottom of the sea, and anchored my immortal soul to its Bishop, causing it to swim above the sea, the world, where all the raging waves, foul weather, tempests and temptations are. But O! then did I see my troubles, trials, and temptations more clearly than ever I had done. As the light appeared all appeared that is out of the light; darkness, death, temptations, the unrighteous, the ungodly; all was manifest and seen in the light.

Passing on, I went among the professors at Duck-ingfield and Manchester, where I stayed awhile, and declared truth among them. There were some convinced who received the Lord's teaching, by which they were confirmed and stood in the truth. But the professors were in a rage, all pleading for sin and imperfection, and could not endure to hear talk of perfection, and of a holy and sinless life. But the Lord's power was over all, though they were chained under darkness and sin, which they pleaded for, and quenched the tender thing in them.

Then came people from far and near to see me; but I was fearful of being drawn out by them; yet I was made to speak, and open things to them. There was one Brown, who had great prophecies and sights upon his death-bed of me. He spoke only of what I should be made instru-mental by the Lord to bring forth. And of others he spoke, that they should come to nothing, which was fulfilled on some, who then were something in show.

When this man was buried a great work of the Lord fell upon me, to the admiration of many, who thought I had been dead, and many came to see me for about four-teen days. I was very much altered in countenance and person, as if my body had been new moulded or changed. My sorrows and troubles began to wear off, and tears of joy dropped from me, so that I could have wept night and day with tears of joy to the Lord, in humility and broken-ness of heart.

I saw into that which was without end, things which cannot be uttered, and of the greatness and infinitude of the love of God, which cannot be expressed by words. For I had been brought through the very ocean of darkness and death, and through and over the power of Satan, by the eternal, glorious power of Christ; even through that darkness was I brought, which covered over all the world, and which chained down all and shut up all in death. The same eternal power of God, which brought me through these things, was that which afterwards shook the nations, priests, professors and people.

Now, after I had had some service in these parts, I went through Derbyshire into my own county, Leicestershire, again, and several tender people were convinced.

Then I heard of a great meeting to be at Leicester, for a dispute, wherein Presbyterians, Independents, Baptists and Common-prayer-men were said to be all concerned. The meeting was in a steeple-house; and thither I was moved by the Lord God to go, and be amongst them. I heard their discourse and reasonings, some being in pews, and the priest in the pulpit; abundance of people being gathered together.

At last one woman asked a question out of Peter, What that birth was, viz., a being born again of incorruptible seed, by the Word of God, that liveth and abideth for ever? And the priest said to her, "I permit not a woman to speak in the church"; though he had before given liberty for any to speak. Whereupon I was wrapped up, as in a rapture, in the Lord's power; and I stepped up and asked the priest, "Dost thou call this (the steeple-house) a church? Or dost thou call this mixed multitude a church?" For the woman asking a question, he ought to have answered it, having given liberty for any to speak.

But, instead of answering me, he asked me what a church was? I told him the church was the pillar and ground of truth, made up of living stones, living members, a spiritual household, which Christ was the head of; but he was not the head of a mixed multitude, or of an old house made up of lime, stones and wood.

This set them all on fire. The priest came down from his pulpit, and others out of their pews, and the dispute there was marred. I went to a great inn, and there disputed the thing with the priests and professors, who were all on fire. But I maintained the true church, and the true head thereof, over their heads, till they all gave out and fled away. One man seemed loving, and appeared for a while to join with me; but he soon turned against me, and joined with a priest in pleading for infant-baptism, though himself had been a Baptist before; so he left me alone. Howbeit, there were several convinced that day; the woman that asked the question was convinced, and her family; and the Lord's power and glory shone over all.

After this I returned into Nottinghamshire again, and went into the Vale of Beavor. As I went, I preached repentance to the people. There were many convinced in the Vale of Beavor, in many towns; for I stayed some weeks amongst them.

Thus the work of the Lord went forward, and many were turned from the darkness to the light, within the compass of these three years, 1646, 1647 and 1648. Divers meetings of Friends, in several places, were then gathered to God's teaching, by his light, Spirit, and power; for the Lord's power broke forth more and more wonderfully.

Now I was come up in spirit through the flaming sword, into the paradise of God. All things were new; and all the creation gave unto me another smell than before, beyond what words can utter. I knew nothing but pureness, and innocency, and righteousness; being renewed into the image of God by Christ Jesus, to the state of Adam, which he was in before he fell. The creation was opened to me; and it was showed me how all things had their names given them according to their nature and virtue.

I was at a stand in my mind whether I should practise physic for the good of mankind, seeing the nature and virtues of things were so opened to me by the Lord. But I was immediately taken up in spirit to see into another or more steadfast state than Adam's innocency, even into a state in Christ Jesus that should never fall. And the Lord showed me that such as were faithful to Him, in the power and light of Christ, should come up into that state in which Adam was before he fell; in which the admirable works of the creation, and the virtues thereof, may be known, through the openings of that divine Word of wisdom and power by which they were made.

Great things did the Lord lead me into, and wonderful depths were opened unto me, beyond what can by words be declared; but as people come into subjection to the Spirit of God, and grow up in the image and power of the Almighty, they may receive the Word of wisdom that opens all things, and come to know the hidden unity in the Eternal Being.

Thus I travelled on in the Lord's service, as He led me. When I came to Nottingham, the mighty power of God was there among Friends. From thence I went to Clawson, in Leicestershire, in the Vale of Beavor; and the mighty power of God appeared there also, in several towns and villages where Friends were gathered.

Abundance was opened concerning these things; how all lay out of the wisdom of God, and out of the righteousness and holiness that man at the first was made in. But as all believe in the Light, and walk in the Light—that Light with which Christ hath enlightened every man that cometh into the world—and become children of the Light, and of the day of Christ, all things, visible and invisible, are seen, by the divine Light of Christ, the spiritual heavenly man, by whom all things were created.

Moreover, when I was brought up into His image in righteousness and holiness, and into the paradise of God He let me see how Adam was made a living soul; and also the stature of Christ, the mystery that had been from ages and generations: which things are hard to be uttered, and cannot be borne by many. For of all the sects in Christendom (so called) that I discoursed with, I found none who could bear to be told that any should come to Adam's perfection—into that image of God, that righteousness and holiness, that Adam was in before he fell; to be clean and pure, without sin, as he was. Therefore how shall they be able to bear being told that any shall grow up to the measure of the stature of the fulness of Christ, when they cannot bear to hear that any shall come, whilst upon earth, into the same power and Spirit that the prophets and apostles were in?—though it be a certain truth that none can understand their writings aright without the same Spirit by which they were written.

Now the Lord God opened to me by His invisible power that every man was enlightened by the divine Light of Christ, and I saw it shine through all; and that they that believed in it came out of condemnation to the Light of life, and became the children of it; but they that hated it, and did not believe in it, were condemned by it, though they made a profession of Christ. This I saw in the pure openings of the Light without the help of any man; neither did I then know where to find it in the Scriptures; though afterwards, searching the Scriptures, I found it. For I saw, in that Light and Spirit which was before the Scriptures were given forth, and which led the holy men of God to give them forth, that all, if they would know God or Christ, or the Scriptures aright, must come to that Spirit by which they that gave them forth were led and taught.

11

AT THE HERMITAGE
OF FATHER SERAPHIM

И таким-то образом благодать
Всесвятого Духа Божия является
в неизреченном свете для всех,
которым Бог являет действие ее.

It is by this ineffable light that the action of the
grace of the Holy Spirit manifests itself to all
those to whom God vouchsafes to reveal it.

———St. Seraphim
The Notes of Motovilov

♦ ♦ ♦

Russia's largest religious population is Eastern Orthodox Christianity, and its most popular saint is the 19th-century Orthodox monk, St. Seraphim of Sarov (1759–1833). Present at St. Seraphim's canonization in 1903 was the last Russian Emperor, Tsar Nicholas II. The fiftieth anniversary of his canonization was solemnly observed in 1953.

St. Seraphim was born during the reign of Elizabeth, daughter of Peter the Great. He was born in the small village of Kursk, the son of a brickmaker. At his baptism, he was given the name Prokhor. When he reached age 17, the family decided he would enter his elder brother's merchant business, but Prokhor had dreamed of the monastic life from an early age. He had studied the lives of past hermits who lived in solitude in the vast forests of the Russian wilderness, and aspired after such a life himself. After a year spent in his brother's shop, he entered the monastery of Sarov, situated near Kursk, on a hill surrounded by dense forest. After a noviate program of eight years, he took his vows and was given the name Seraphim.

After many years of active participation in the communal life of the monastery, Seraphim, now a priest 31 years old, again felt the call of the solitary life of a hermit. He asked for and was granted permission to retire to a remote house belonging to the monastery. Seraphim loved his new life of poverty and solitude. Although still a young man, he was said to be prematurely aged and weak, but always joyful, constantly singing or repeating the "Jesus Prayer" as he tended his garden. He was known to feed many of the wild animals including a huge bear who was seen lying quietly at his feet.

Before his retirement to the hut, various supernatural phenomena had been observed around him. A light had once shown on his face, instances of healing had occurred, it was told he had divine visitations. These stories spread and he was now becoming more and more well-known. His forest solitude was therefore often interrupted with uninvited guests who came to seek his spiritual advice.

In September of 1804, Seraphim had more uninvited guests, this time of quite a different nature. Three peasants from a neighboring village, drawn by rumors of hidden treasure in the forest, demanded money from the hermit. They beat him unconscious and ransacked the hut, but found only a few potatoes and a sack of stones which served as a mattress. Seraphim was beaten nearly to death and his convalescence took several months. As a result of his injuries, he remained a hunchback the rest of his life. The attackers were later apprehended, but pardoned at Seraphim's request.

When he returned to the forest, he required the aid of a staff or cane to walk. He now took a vow of silence and received no visitors for a period of five years. At last he was instructed in a spiritual vision to abandon his seclusion and receive visitors. Seraphim, now over 60, became a "Staretz," or spiritual director. Once the door of his cell was opened, large crowds of visitors became a daily occurrence. Soon there were many recorded instances of clairvoyance, prophecy, and healing of the sick. The road to the Sarov Monastery became crowded with carriages, coaches, carts, and pilgrims on foot all traveling to visit the holy man.

One day a rich young man named Nicholas Motovilov arrived at the monastery, carried by five servants. He owned large estates in three provinces of central Russia and held an administrative post, but had been paralyzed and bedridden with an unknown ailment for three years. Seraphim commanded him to walk, which he was miraculously able to do and was thereafter completely healed.

Motovilov soon became a special friend to the Staretz and was put in charge of the community now developing around the monastery. He kept a journal of his many meetings with Staretz Seraphim. These memoirs became known as *The Notes of Motovilov* and were published in 1903, sixty years after Seraphim's death and the year of his canonization. They contain the accounts of many wonderful experiences. From the *Notes*, we reprint an account of one special meeting related by Motovilov. It is November 1831, just a month or two after his healing. He is told that the Staretz is calling for him and waiting for him in his cell.

♦   ♦   ♦

To anyone who has not experienced the delight and fulfillment that come to a man on whom the Spirit of God rests, my words may seem empty and my story fantastic; however, I testify that everything I am going to state is the pure truth without any exaggeration and that it is only a very faint reproduction of what I felt.

'So it was Thursday; it was a grey day and the ground was covered with a thick layer of snow. Great flakes were still falling when Father Seraphim began talking to me in the glade close by his Near Hermitage, on the banks of the Sarovka. He seated me on a recently-felled tree-trunk and sat down opposite me.

' "The Lord has shown me," he said, "that when you were a child you wanted to know the goal of the Christian life and that you had put this question to a number of eminent ecclesiastics." I must confess that this question had indeed weighed heavily on my mind since I was twelve, and that I had often asked it without receiving a satisfactory reply.

' "Yet no one," continued Father Seraphim, "told you anything definite. They instructed you to go to church, to pray, to do good works, telling you that there lay the goal of the Christian life. Some of them even said to you: 'Don't search into things that are beyond you.' Well, miserable servant of God that I am, I am going to try to explain to you what this goal is. Prayer, fasting, works of mercy—all this is very good, but it represents only the means, not the end of the Christian life. The true end is the acquisition of the Holy Spirit."

' "This Holy Spirit, the All-powerful, is given to us on condition that we ourselves know how to acquire him. He takes up his abode in us and prepares in our souls and bodies a dwelling-place for the Father, according to the word of God: 'I will live in them and move among them, and I will be their God and they shall be my people' (2 Cor. 6:16).

' "The grace of the Holy Spirit, given at baptism in the name of the Father, and of the Son, and of the Holy Spirit, continues to shine in our heart as divine light in spite of our falls and the darkness of our soul. It is this grace that cries in us to the Father: 'Abba, Father!' and who reclothes the soul in the incorruptible garment woven for us by the Holy Spirit.

' "To give you more light on this subject, friend of God, I must tell you that the Lord often revealed the workings of this grace in those whom he sanctified and illumined. Remember Moses after his conversation with God on Mount Sinai: the people could not look at him because of the dazzling light that shone from his face and he could only be with them when he covered it with a veil (Ex. 34:30–35). And recall our Lord's transfiguration as well: 'His face shone like the sun, and his garments became white as light' and 'the disciples fell on their faces and were filled with awe' (Matt. 17:2, 6). When Moses and Elijah appeared illumined by this light we are told that a cloud came and covered the disciples with its shade to enable them to bear the brightness of that divine grace which blinded their eyes. Well, it is by this ineffable light that the action of the grace of the Holy Spirit manifests itself to all those to whom God vouchsafes to reveal it."

' "But how", I asked him, "can I know that I am within this grace of the Holy Spirit?"

' "It is very easy, friend of God," replied Father Seraphim, "because everything is easy to those who have obtained understanding. It is our misfortune that we don't seek after the Wisdom that comes from God. The apostles, having acquired this Wisdom, always knew whether or not the Spirit of God rested in them; when they possessed it they were sure that their work was holy and acceptable to God. With this basic certainty they were able to write in their letters: 'It seemed good to the Holy Spirit and to us' (Acts 15:28) as being a statement of the unshakeable truth necessary to the faithful. So you see, friend of God, it is very easy!"

Then I answered, "I don't quite grasp how it is possible to be absolutely sure of living in God's Spirit. How can it be proved?"

The Staretz reiterated: "Friend of God, I've already told you that it's very easy: I've told you that some men found themselves filled with the Holy Spirit and were able to be convinced of his presence; what more do you want?"

' "How I long to understand completely!"

Then Father Seraphim gripped me firmly by the shoulders and said: "My friend, both of us, at this moment, are in the Holy Spirit, you and I. Why won't you look at me?"

' "I can't look at you, Father, because the light flashing from your eyes and face is brighter than the sun and I'm dazzled!"

' "Don't be afraid, friend of God, you yourself are shining just like I am; you too are now in the fullness of the grace of the Holy Spirit, otherwise you wouldn't be able to see me as you do."

'And, leaning towards me, Father Seraphim said quietly: "Thank the Lord for his ineffable goodness: you may have noticed that I didn't even make the sign of the cross; only in my heart I said this prayer to the Lord: 'Lord, grant him the grace of seeing clearly, with the eyes of the flesh, that outpouring of your Spirit which you vouchsafe to your servants when you condescend to reveal yourself to them in the reflection of your glory.' My friend, the Lord granted it instantly—merely at poor Seraphim's prayer. How we must thank him for this gladness that he has given us both! As a mother comforts her children, so does he fill our penitent hearts. So, my friend, why not look at me? Come on, look, don't be afraid, for the Lord is with us!"

'Then I looked at the Staretz and was panic-stricken. Picture, in the sun's orb, in the most dazzling brightness of its noon-day shining, the face of a man who is talking to you. You see his lips moving, the expression in his eyes, you hear his voice, you feel his arms round your shoulders, and yet you see neither his arms, nor his body, nor his face, you lose all sense of yourself, you can see only the blinding light which spreads everywhere, lighting up the layer of snow covering the glade, and igniting the flakes that are falling on us both like white powder.

' "What do you feel?" asked Father Seraphim.

' "An amazing well-being!" I replied.

' "But what exactly is it?"

' "I feel a great calm in my soul, a peace which no words can express."

' "This is the peace, friend of God, which the Lord promised to his disciples when he said: 'Peace I leave with you, my peace I give to you; not as the world gives do I give to you' (John 14:27). It is that peace which the Apostle calls 'the peace which passes all understanding' (Phil. 4:7). This is what is filling your heart now. And what else do you feel?"

' "A strange, unknown delight."

' "Yes, that's how it is with those delights which the Psalmist describes, saying that the sons of men will be given drink from the river of God's delights and will feast on the abundance of God's house (Ps. 36:8). These delights fill us with an ineffable blessedness that melts our heart, a blessedness that is beyond words. What more do you feel?"

' "An amazing happiness fills my heart."

'Father Seraphim went on: "When the Holy Spirit descends and fills the soul with the plenitude of his presence, then we experience that joy which Christ described, the joy which the world cannot take away. However, the joy you now feel in your heart is nothing compared to that which Paul the Apostle describes: 'What no eye has seen, nor ear heard, nor the heart of man conceived, what God has prepared for those who love him' (1 Cor. 2:9). The first fruits of that joy are already given us and if our soul is even now filled with such glad sweetness, what words can express the joy laid up in heaven for those who sorrow here below? And you too, friend of God, have had grief in your life; see how joyfully God has already comforted you in this world. Do you feel anything else, my friend?"

' "I'm amazingly warm."

' "Warm? What are you saying, my friend? We are in the depths of the forest, in mid-winter, the snow lies under our feet and is settling on our clothes. How can you be warm?"

' " It's the warmth one feels in a hot bath."

' "Does it smell like that?"

' "Oh no, nothing on earth can be compared to this! There's no scent in all the world like this one!"

' "I know," said Father Seraphim, smiling, "It's the same with me. I'm only questioning you to find out what you're discovering. It is indeed true, friend of God, that no scent on earth can be compared with this fragrance, because it comes from the Holy Spirit. By the way, you've just told me that you've been feeling the warmth of a hot bath, but look: the snow settling on us isn't melting, neither on you nor on me. That shows that the warmth isn't in the air but is within us. This is what the Holy Spirit causes us to ask God for when we cry to him: 'Kindle in us the fire of the Holy Spirit!' Warmed by it, hermits are not afraid of winter hardship, protected as they are by the mantle of grace which the Holy Spirit has woven for them. This is as it should be, for divine grace comes to live in our hearts, within us. Didn't the Lord say: 'The kingdom of God is within you' (Luke 17:21)? This kingdom is just the grace of the Holy Spirit, living in us, warming us, enlightening us, filling the air with his scent, delighting us with his fragrance and rejoicing our hearts with an ineffable gladness. At this moment we are with those whom the Lord mentions as not tasting death before they see the kingdom of God come with power (Luke 9:27; Mark 9:1). Now you know, my friend, what it's like to be in the fullness of the Holy Spirit, as Macarius the Great writes: 'It was as though I were engulfed in the outpouring of the Holy Spirit.' This is what we are filled with today, in spite of our unworthiness. Friend of God, I don't think you'll ask again how to recognize the presence of the Holy Spirit. Treasure this memory of the revelation given you of the fathomless loving-kindness of God who has visited you today."

' "Father," I replied, "I'm not sure that the Lord will enable me to keep the remembrance of his mercy vivid for ever; I'm so unworthy."

' "I'm quite sure," the father replied, "that God will help you to remember these moments for ever, otherwise in his goodness he would not have been so swift to answer poor Seraphim's prayer. Besides, this revelation hasn't been given you just for your own sake but, through you, to the whole world, so that, confirmed by the action of grace, you may use it in serving your neighbour.

' "The fact that I am a monk and you a layman doesn't make any difference. What counts in God's eyes is true faith in him and in his only Son. It is for this that the grace of the Holy Spirit is given us; the Lord seeks hearts overflowing with love for him and their neighbour, and this is the throne where he would sit and reveal himself in the fullness of his glory. 'My son, give me your heart', he says (Prov. 23:26). For in the heart he builds the kingdom of God." '

12

THE HIMALAYAS WITHIN

My body became immovably rooted; breath was
drawn out of my lungs as if by some huge magnet. Soul and mind instantly lost their physical
bondage and streamed out like a fluid piercing
light from my every pore. The flesh was as
though dead, yet in my intense awareness I
knew that never before had I been fully
alive. . . .

——Paramahansa Yogananda
Autobiography of a Yogi

♦ ♦ ♦

Mukunda Lal Ghosh was born in 1893 in northern India near the Himalaya Mountains. Soon after graduating high school, he met his beloved guru, Swami Sri Yukteswar, in a town near Calcutta. But much to Mukunda's chagrin, Sri Yukteswar instructed him not to join the hermitage right away but to continue his studies at Calcutta University. The guru predicted that Mukunda would some day go to the West and would be better received bearing a university degree. Always the reluctant student, Mukunda spent little time in class but managed to "miraculously" pass his final exams. Upon graduation, he was initiated into the Swami Order by his guru, in 1915, and given the name Yogananda. Five years later he received a rare invitation from the West—to address the International Congress of Religious Liberals in Boston. Yogananda traveled widely in America and settled in Los Angeles. There he founded the Self-Realization Fellowship, which exists to this day. He died in Los Angeles on March 7, 1952.

Yogananda's memoirs, entitled *Autobiography of a Yogi,* have become a classic of spiritual literature. This book introduced the profound mysteries of yoga to Western audiences as never before. Yogananda does not hesitate to share with his readers the truly extraordinary events of his life and his incredible experiences in higher consciousness. His struggles for enlightenment begin in earnest quite early. As a very young child, he feels irresistibly drawn to the Himalaya Mountains. Twice he runs away from home toward the holy mounts in search of great spiritual adventure. But his efforts are thwarted each time by his older, more worldly-minded brother, Ananta. Even after meeting his guru, Mukunda's sights are focused toward the Himalayas. Finally, after a last ill-fated journey toward the mountains, Mukunda's true desires are fulfilled in a most unexpected way. The following tale is a compilation of excerpts from five chapters of Yogananda's autobiography.

♦ ♦ ♦

I was born on January 5, 1893, in Gorakhpur in northeastern India near the Himalaya Mountains. There my first eight years were passed. We were eight children: four boys and four girls. Father and Mother were Bengalis, of the *Kshatriya* caste [the second caste, originally that of rulers and warriors]. Father was kind, grave, at times stern. Loving him dearly, we children yet observed a certain reverential distance. An outstanding mathematician and logician, he was guided principally by his intellect. My mother's greatest desire was the marriage of my elder brother. "Ah, when I behold the face of Ananta's wife, I shall find heaven on this earth!" I frequently heard Mother express in these words her strong Indian sentiment for family continuity.

I was about eleven years old at the time of Ananta's betrothal. Mother was in Calcutta, joyously supervising the wedding preparations. Father and I alone remained at our home in Bareilly. Intense pangs of longing for God assailed me. I felt drawn to the Himalayas. One of my cousins, fresh from a period of travel in the holy hills, visited us in Bareilly. I listened eagerly to his tales about the high mountain abode of yogis and swamis.

"Let us run away to the Himalayas." My suggestion one day to Dwarka Prasad, the young son of our landlord in Bareilly, fell on unsympathetic ears. He revealed my plan to my elder brother. Instead of laughing lightly over this impractical scheme of a small boy, Ananta made it a definite point to ridicule me.

"Where is your orange robe? You can't be a swami without that!"

But I was inexplicably thrilled by his words. They brought me a clear picture: that of myself as a monk, roaming about India. I fled that afternoon toward Naini Tal in the Himalayan foothills. Ananta gave determined chase; I was forced to return sadly to Bareilly.

[A few years later, now a high school student, Mukunda again attempts to visit the Himalayas.]

"Leave your classroom on some trifling pretext. And engage a hackney carriage. Stop in the lane where no one in my house can see you." These were my final instructions to Amar Mitter, a highschool friend who planned to accompany me to the Himalayas. We had chosen the following day for our flight. Precautions were necessary, as my brother Ananta exercised a vigilant eye. He was determined to foil the plans of escape that he suspected were uppermost in my mind. I hoped to find, amid the Himalayan snows, the master whose face often appeared to me in visions.

The family was living now in Calcutta, where Father had been permanently transferred. Following the patriarchal Indian custom, Ananta had brought his bride to live in our home, now at 4 Gurpar Road. There in a small attic room I engaged in daily meditations and prepared my mind for the divine search.

The memorable morning arrived with inauspicious rain. Hearing the wheels of Amar's carriage in the road, I hastily tied together a blanket, a pair of sandals, two loincloths, a string of prayer beads, Lahiri Mahasaya's picture, and a copy of the *Bhagavad Gita*. This bundle I threw from my third-story window. I ran down the steps and passed my uncle, buying fish at the door.

"What is the excitement?" His gaze roved suspiciously over my person.

I gave him a noncommittal smile and walked to the lane. Retrieving my bundle, I joined Amar with conspiratorial caution. We drove to Chandni Chauk, a merchandise center. For months we had been saving our tiffin money to buy English clothes. Knowing that my clever brother could easily play the part of a detective, we thought to outwit him by wearing European garb.

On the way to the station, we stopped for my cousin, Jotin Ghosh, whom I called Jatinda. He was a new convert, longing for a guru in the Himalayas. He donned the new suit we had in readiness. Well-camouflaged, we hoped! A deep elation possessed our hearts.

"All we need now are canvas shoes." I led my companions to a shop displaying rubber-soled footwear. "Articles of leather, got only through the slaughter of animals, should be absent on this holy trip." I halted on the street to remove the leather cover from my *Bhagavad Gita*, and the leather straps from my English-made *sola topee* (helmet).

At the station we bought tickets to Burdwan, where we planned to transfer for Hardwar in the Himalayan foothills. As soon as the train, like ourselves, was in flight, I gave utterance to a few of my glorious anticipations.

"Just imagine!" I ejaculated. "We shall be initiated by the masters and experience the trance of cosmic consciousness. Our flesh will be charged with such magnetism that wild animals of the Himalayas will come tamely near us. Tigers will be no more than meek house-cats awaiting our caresses!"

This remark—picturing a prospect I considered entrancing, both metaphorically and literally—brought an enthusiastic smile from Amar. But Jatinda averted his gaze, directing it through the window at the scampering landscape.

"Let the money be divided in three portions." Jatinda broke a long silence with this suggestion. "Each of us should buy his own ticket at Burdwan. Thus no one at the station will surmise that we are running away together."

I unsuspectingly agreed. At dusk our train stopped at Burdwan. Jatinda entered the ticket office; Amar and I sat on the platform. We waited fifteen minutes, then made unavailing inquiries. Searching in all directions, we shouted Jatinda's name with the urgency of fright. But he had faded into the dark unknown surrounding the little station.

I was completely unnerved, shocked to a peculiar numbness. That God would countenance this depressing episode! The romantic occasion of my first carefully planned flight after Him was cruelly marred.

"Amar, we must return home." I was weeping like a child. "Jatinda's callous departure is an ill omen. This trip is doomed to failure."

"Is this your love for the Lord? Can't you stand the little test of a treacherous companion?"

Through Amar's suggestion of a divine test, my heart steadied itself. We refreshed ourselves with famous Burdwan sweetmeats, *sitabhog* (food for the goddess) and *motichur* (nuggets of sweet pearl). In a few hours we entrained for Hardwar, via Bareilly. Changing trains the following day at Moghul Serai, we discussed a vital matter as we waited on the platform.

"Amar, we may soon be closely questioned by railroad officials. I am not underrating my brother's ingenuity! No matter what the outcome, I will not speak untruth."

"All I ask of you, Mukunda, is to keep still. Don't laugh or grin while I am talking."

At this moment a European station-agent accosted me. He waved a telegram whose import I immediately grasped.

"Are you running away from home in anger?"

"No!" I was glad his choice of words permitted me to make emphatic reply. Not anger but "divinest melancholy" was responsible, I knew, for my unconventional behavior.

The official then turned to Amar. The duel of wits that followed hardly permitted me to maintain the counseled stoic gravity.

"Where is the third boy?" The man injected a full ring of authority into his voice. "Come now—speak the truth!"

"Sir, I notice you are wearing eyeglasses. Can't you see that we are only two?" Amar smiled impudently. "I am not a magician; I can't conjure up a third boy."

The official, noticeably disconcerted by this impertinence, sought a new field of attack. "What is your name?"

"I am called Thomas. I am the son of an English mother and a converted Christian Indian father."

"What is you friend's name?"

"I call him Thompson."

By this time my inward mirth had reached a zenith; I unceremoniously made for the train, which was providentially whistling for departure. Amar followed with the official, who was credulous and obliging enough to put us into a European compartment. It evidently pained him to think of two half-English boys traveling in the section allotted to natives. After his polite exit, I lay back on the seat and laughed uproariously. Amar wore an expression of blithe satisfaction at having outwitted a veteran European official.

On the platform I had contrived to read the telegram. From my brother Ananta, it went thus: "Three Bengali boys in English clothes running away from home toward Hardwar via Moghul Serai. Please detain them until my arrival. Ample reward for your services."

"Amar, I told you not to leave marked timetables in your home." My glance was reproachful. "Brother must have found one there."

While our train stood in a station that night, and I was half asleep, Amar was awakened by another questioning official. He, too, fell a victim to the hybrid charms of "Thomas" and "Thompson." The train bore us triumphantly into a dawn arrival at Hardwar. The majestic mountains loomed invitingly in the distance. We dashed through the station and entered the freedom of city crowds. Our first act was to change into native costume, as Ananta had somehow penetrated our European disguise. A premonition of capture weighed on my mind.

Deeming it advisable to leave Hardwar at once, we bought tickets to proceed north to Rishikesh, a soil long hallowed by the feet of many masters. I had already boarded the train, while Amar lagged on the platform. He was brought to an abrupt halt by a shout from a policeman. An unwelcome guardian, the officer escorted Amar and me to a police-station bungalow and took charge of our money. He explained courteously that it was his duty to hold us until my elder brother arrived.

So near the Himalayas and yet, in our captivity, so far, I told Amar I felt doubly impelled to seek freedom.

"Let us slip away when opportunity offers. We can go on foot to holy Rishikesh." I smiled encouragingly.

But my companion had turned pessimist as soon as the stalwart prop of our money had been taken from us.

"If we started a trek over such dangerous jungle land, we should finish, not in the city of saints, but in the stomachs of tigers!"

Ananta and Amar's brother arrived after three days. Amar greeted his relative with affectionate relief. I was unreconciled; Ananta got no more from me than a severe upbraiding.

[After high school, Mukunda meets his guru, Sri Yukteswar. Still, his yearnings to visit the Himalayas are undiminished. One day, he asks his guru:]

"Please permit me to go to the Himalayas."

"Many hillmen live in the Himalayas, yet possess no God perception." My guru's answer came slowly and simply. "Wisdom is better sought from a man of realization than from an inert mountain."

Ignoring Master's plain hint that he, and not a hill, was my teacher, I repeated my plea. Sri Yukteswar vouchsafed no reply. I took his silence for consent—a precarious but convenient interpretation.

In my Calcutta home that evening, I busied myself with travel preparations. Tying a few articles inside a blanket, I remembered a similar bundle, surreptitiously dropped from my attic window a few years earlier. I wondered if this were to be another ill-starred flight toward the Himalayas. The first time my spiritual elation had been high; tonight my conscience smote me at the thought of leaving my guru.

The following morning I sought out Behari Pundit, my Sanskrit professor at Scottish Church College.

"Sir, you have told me of your friendship with a great disciple of Lahiri Mahasaya. Please give me his address."

"You mean Ram Gopal Muzumdar. I call him the 'sleepless saint.' He is always awake in an ecstatic consciousness. His home is in Ranbajpur, near Tarakeswar."

I thanked the pundit and entrained immediately for Tarakeswar. I hoped to silence my misgivings by getting permission from the "sleepless saint" to engage myself in lonely meditation in the Himalayas. Behari Pundit had told me that Ram Gopal had received illumination after many years of *Kriya Yoga* practice in isolated caves in Bengal. [But upon finding the saint, Mukunda does not receive the instructions he expects:]

"Young yogi, I see you are running away from your master. He has everything you need; you should return to him." He added, "Mountains cannot be your guru"—the same thought that Sri Yukteswar had expressed two days earlier.

"Masters are under no cosmic compulsion to live on mountains only." My companion glanced at me quizzically. "The Himalayas in India and Tibet have no monopoly on saints. What one does not trouble to find within will not be discovered by transporting the body hither and yon. As soon as the devotee is *willing* to go even to the ends of the earth for spiritual enlightenment, his guru appears nearby.

"Are you able to have a little room where you can close the door and be alone?"

"Yes."

"That is your cave. That is your sacred mountain. That is where you will find the kingdom of God."

His simple words instantaneously banished my lifelong obsession for the Himalayas.

I entrained happily for Calcutta. My travels ended, not in the lofty mountains, but in the Himalayan presence of my master. . . .

I am here, Guruji." My shamefacedness spoke more eloquently for me.

"Let us go to the kitchen and find something to eat." Sri Yukteswar's manner was as casual as though hours and not days had separated us.

"Master, I must have disappointed you by my abrupt departure from my duties here; I thought you might be angry with me."

"No, of course not! Wrath springs only from thwarted desires. I do not expect anything from others, so their actions cannot be in opposition to wishes of mine. I would not use you for my own ends; I am happy only in your own true happiness."

"Sir, one hears of divine love in a vague way, but today I am indeed having a concrete example of it from your angelic self! In the world, even a father does not easily forgive his son if he leaves his parent's business without warning. But you show not the slightest vexation, though you must have been put to great inconvenience by the many unfinished tasks I left behind."

A few mornings later I made my way to Master's empty sitting room. I planned to meditate, but my laudable purpose was unshared by disobedient thoughts. They scattered like birds before the hunter.

"Mukunda!" Sri Yukteswar's voice sounded from a distant balcony.

I felt as rebellious as my thoughts. "Master always urges me to meditate," I muttered to myself. "He should not disturb me when he knows why I came to his room."

He summoned me again; I remained obstinately silent. The third time his tone held rebuke.

"Sir, I am meditating," I shouted protestingly.

"I know how you are meditating," my guru called out, "with your mind distributed like leaves in a storm! Come here to me."

Thwarted and exposed, I made my way sadly to his side.

"Poor boy, mountains cannot give you what you want." Master spoke caressingly, comfortingly. His calm gaze was unfathomable. "Your heart's desire shall be fulfilled."

Sri Yukteswar seldom indulged in riddles; I was bewildered. He struck gently on my chest above the heart.

My body became immovably rooted; breath was drawn out of my lungs as if by some huge magnet. Soul and mind instantly lost their physical bondage and streamed out like a fluid piercing light from my every pore. The flesh was as though dead, yet in my intense awareness I knew that never before had I been fully alive. My sense of identity was no longer narrowly confined to a body but embraced the circumambient atoms. People on distant streets seemed to be moving gently over my own remote periphery. The roots of plants and trees appeared through a dim transparency of the soil; I discerned the inward flow of their sap.

The whole vicinity lay bare before me. My ordinary frontal vision was now changed to a vast spherical sight, simultaneously all-perceptive. Through the back of my head I saw men strolling far down Rai Ghat Lane, and noticed also a white cow that was leisurely approaching. When she reached the open ashram gate, I observed her as though with my two physical eyes. After she had passed behind the brick wall of the courtyard, I saw her clearly still.

All objects within my panoramic gaze trembled and vibrated like quick motion pictures. My body, Master's, the pillared courtyard, the furniture and floor, the trees and sunshine, occasionally became violently agitated, until all melted into a luminescent sea; even as sugar crystals, thrown into a glass of water, dissolve after being shaken. The unifying light alternated with materializations of form, the metamorphoses revealing the law of cause and effect in creation.

An oceanic joy broke upon calm endless shores of my soul. The Spirit of God, I realized, is exhaustless Bliss; His body is countless tissues of light. A swelling glory within me began to envelop towns, continents, the earth, solar and stellar systems, tenuous nebulae, and floating universes. The entire cosmos, gently luminous, like a city seen afar at night, glimmered within the infinitude of my being. The dazzling light beyond the sharply etched global outlines faded slightly at the farthest edges; there I saw a mellow radiance, ever undiminished. It was indescribably subtle; the planetary pictures were formed of a grosser light.

The divine dispersion of rays poured from an Eternal Source, blazing into galaxies, transfigured with ineffable auras. Again and again I saw the creative beams condense into constellations, then resolve into sheets of transparent flame. By rhythmic reversion, sextillion worlds passed into diaphanous luster, then fire became firmament.

I cognized the center of the empyrean as a point of intuitive perception in my heart. Irradiating splendor issued from my nucleus to every part of the universal structure. Blissful *amrita*, nectar of immortality, pulsated through me with a quicksilverlike fluidity. The creative voice of God I heard resounding as *Aum*, the vibration of the Cosmic Motor.

Suddenly the breath returned to my lungs. With a disappointment almost unbearable, I realized that my infinite immensity was lost. Once more I was limited to the humiliating cage of a body, not easily accommodative to the Spirit. Like a prodigal child, I had run away from my macrocosmic home and had imprisoned myself in a narrow microcosm.

My guru was standing motionless before me; I started to prostrate myself at his holy feet in gratitude for his having bestowed on me the experience in cosmic consciousness that I had long passionately sought. He held me upright and said quietly:

"You must not get overdrunk with ecstasy. Much work yet remains for you in the world. Come, let us sweep the balcony floor; then we shall walk by the Ganges."

I fetched a broom; Master, I knew, was teaching me the secret of balance living. The soul must stretch over the cosmogonic abysses, while the body performs its daily duties.

When Sri Yukteswar and I set out later for a stroll, I was still entranced in unspeakable rapture. I saw our bodies as two astral pictures, moving over a road by the river whose essence was sheer light.

"It is the Spirit of God that actively sustains every form and force in the universe; yet He is transcendental and aloof in the blissful uncreated void beyond the worlds of vibratory phenomena," Master explained. "Those who attain Self-realization on earth live a similar twofold existence. Conscientiously performing their work in the world, they are yet immersed in an inward beatitude.

"The Lord has created all men from the illimitable joy of His being. Though they are painfully cramped by the body, God nevertheless expects that men made in His image shall ultimately rise above all sense identifications and reunite with Him."

The cosmic vision left many permanent lessons. By daily stilling my thoughts, I could win release from the delusive conviction that my body was a mass of flesh and bones, traversing the hard soil of matter. The breath and the restless mind, I saw, are like storms that lash the ocean of light into waves of material forms—earth, sky, human beings, animals, birds, trees. No perception of the Infinite as One Light can be had except by calming those storms.

As often as I quieted the two natural tumults, I beheld the multitudinous waves of creation melt into one lucent sea; even as the waves of the ocean, when a tempest subsides, serenely dissolve into unity.

A master bestows the divine experience of cosmic consciousness when his disciple, by meditation, has strengthened his mind to a degree where the vast vistas would not overwhelm him. Mere intellectual willingness or open-mindedness is not enough. Only adequate enlargement of consciousness by yoga practice and devotional *bhakti* can prepare one to absorb the liberating shock of omnipresence.

The divine experience comes with a natural inevitability to the sincere devotee. His intense craving begins to pull at God with an irresistible force. The Lord as the Cosmic Vision is drawn by that magnetic ardor into the seeker's range of consciousness.

A yogi who through perfect meditation has merged his consciousness with the Creator perceives the cosmical essence as light; to him there is no difference between the light rays composing water and the light rays composing land. Free from matter-consciousness, free from the three dimensions of space and the fourth dimension of time, a master transfers his body of light with equal ease over or through the light rays of earth, water, fire, and air.

Long concentration on the liberating spiritual eye has enabled the yogi to destroy all delusions concerning matter and its gravitational weight; he sees the universe as the Lord created it: an essentially undifferentiated mass of light.

PART III

SCIENCE

13

RIDING A BEAM OF LIGHT
IN MODERN PHYSICS

Wenn ich einem Lichtstrahl nacheile mit der Geschwindigkeit c (Lichtgeschwindigkeit im Vacuum), so sollte ich einen solchen Lichtstrahl als ruhendes, räumlich oszillatorisches elektromagnetisches Feld wahrnehmen. So etwas scheint es aber nicht zu geben . . . . Man sieht, dass in diesem Paradoxon der Keim zur speziellen Relativitätstheorie schon enthalten ist.

If I pursue a beam of light with the velocity c (velocity of light in a vacuum), I should observe such a beam of light as a spatially oscillatory electrogmagnetic field at rest. However, there seems to be no such thing . . . . One sees that in this paradox the germ of the special relativity theory is already contained.

——Albert Einstein
Autobiographical Notes

♦   ♦   ♦

In 1895, a 16-year-old German student named Albert Einstein made a curious reflection: "What would the universe look like riding on a beam of light?" For Einstein, this inquiry was at once spiritual and scientific. He would later assert: "I maintain that the cosmic religious feeling is the strongest and noblest motive for scientific research."[1] Einstein did not put aside his wonderment, but pursued the riddles of light for nine years. His efforts eventually led to a major breakthrough in physics—the special theory of relativity. This theory, however, did not fully solve the mystery of light. Throughout the subsequent development of modern physics, light remained at center stage. As stated by Richard Morris: "The fundamental theories on which all modern physics is based—relativity and quantum mechanics—grew directly out of attempts to understand the nature of light."[2] In this chapter, we trace the history of the scientific investigation into the mystery of light and how this investigation culminated in a totally new and unexpected view of the universe. The discoveries of 20th century physics led science to the very boundary of the objective, physical world, and forced it to postulate the existence of a higher-dimensional realm beyond the material world of time-space. In that higher realm, the speed of light is transcended and all things are connected simultaneously. That realm is the source of all quantized matter, and (according to one of today's top physicists) may be the source of "life" and consciousness as well. These unexpected findings have prompted a number of this century's top physicists to publish their views on the subject of higher consciousness. This chapter reprints some of their

---

[1]Albert Einstein, quoted in Renee Weber, *Dialogues with Scientists and Sages: The Search for Unity* (London & New York: Routledge and Kegan Paul, 1986), p. 17.
[2]Richard Morris, *Light* (Indianapolis: Bobbs-Merrill, 1979) p. 2.

views and ends with a discussion on the mystical experience of the inner light from the viewpoint of modern physics.

◆   ◆   ◆

Scientific understandings of light have only recently emerged from a very long history of *mis*understandings. The first recorded theories on light held that light rays somehow originate in the eye. The ancient Greeks, Romans, and Hindus all independently arrived at this same bizarre notion. For centuries thereafter, there were no advances whatsoever on the subject. Finally, in the 17th century, Descartes successfully formulated the relatively obvious and elementary laws of the reflection and refraction of light. The modern theory of light had begun, but there were still many formidable challenges and major goof-ups ahead.

It was Galileo who initiated science's serious attempts to measure the *speed* of light. The instruments of the time were somewhat lacking in the necessary refinement, but Galileo made a brave attempt. He stationed two assistants atop distant hills, about one mile apart, armed with burning lanterns. As his assistants covered and uncovered their lanterns, Galileo watched for clues to light's transit time. He had apparently not guessed (as present-day scientist Nick Herbert has pointed out), that the speed of light is such that in one second it can circle the entire earth more than seven times.[3] The interval Galileo had crudely attempted to measure is less than a hundred thousandth of a second.[4]

[3]Nick Herbert, *Faster than Light* (New York: New American Library, 1988), p. 9.
[4]Timothy Ferris, *Coming of Age in the Milky Way* (New York: William Morrow, 1988), p. 179.

A few years after Galileo's velocity fiasco, Sir Isaac Newton took up the study of light and, with prism in hand, experimentally established the fact that white light is a composite of all colors. Newton further hypothesized that light consists of a beam of submicroscopic particles, a theory supported by the observable fact that light travels in straight lines. But this seemingly logical idea began a fundamental controversy that would require hundreds of years and several top scientists to resolve.

One of the first dissenting voices to Newton's particle theory belonged to the Dutch scientist Christian Huygens. Huygens presented arguments to the French Academy in 1678 showing that light could not be made up of particles. He maintained that light was propogated as waves, similar to sound waves, which are obviously not particles. But the available evidence at the time was inconsequential and the particle theory won out, due mostly to Newton's unassailable reputation.

The wave theory was banished for over a hundred years before new experimental evidence forced a reopening of the case. In 1801 an English physician named Thomas Young presented a lecture before the English Royal Society describing an experiment he had performed with light. In his work as a physician, Young had discovered the biological cause of astigmatism. His interest in the human eye had led to the experiment with light. It is set up very simply. Place three screens parallel to each other, the first screen containing a pinhole, the second screen containing two slits and the last screen solid. When a beam of light is passed through the pinhole, on through the two slits, and onto the last screen, the expected result would be two distinct lighted areas on the last screen. However, this is not the case; rather a pattern of light and dark areas appear across the whole screen. This "interference pattern," as it is called, can only be explained by the wave theory of light. All waves, such as water, sound, etc., have crests (their high points) and troughs (their low points). When the crest of one wave meets the crest of another wave going in the same direction, the waves will combine and intensify. But when the crest of one wave meets the trough of another, the waves will cancel each other out. In the case of light waves meeting after passing through the two slits, any combined crests produce brighter areas, any combined crests and troughs produce darkness. The wave interference pattern on the last screen would not appear if light was a stream of particles, and thus is established Young's proof for the wave theory. We will return to this "double-slit" experiment a little later when the quantum theory adds a mind-boggling twist.

Young's lecture was attacked and ridiculed, but further evidence was soon forthcoming and Newton's particle theory was at last defeated. It was now official: light consisted of waves. But the mystery had in fact only deepened—no one could say just what was waving. Sound waves are vibrations of the air, and in the vacuum of space sound cannot exist. But light clearly reaches us from distant stars through empty space. This fact necessitated the invention of the famous "luminiferous ether." The ether supposedly filled all space and provided the medium for light's transit. For the next hundred years a great many scientists went on the wild goose chase of experimentally detecting the ether. A peculiar trend was already being established—the more that became known about light, the more inexplicable it seemed.

While the search was going on for the ether, much progress was made on determining the speed of light. Astronomical observations of the moons of Jupiter, the parallax of stars, and ingenious experiments on earth all confirmed the amazing figure of 186,000 miles per second.

In the meantime, two other mysteries were being investigated: magnetism and electricity. An intimate connection between these two forces was first established in 1820 when a coil of wire carrying an electric charge was observed to produce a magnetic field. Conversely, magnets were demonstrated to produce electrical effects. The Scottish theoretical physicist James Maxwell brought together the various studies of electricity and magnetism into a single theory now called electromagnetism. Maxwell was a mathematical physicist. His tools were pen and paper. His work is one of many intriguing instances in which mathematical equations successfully predicted physical laws before they were otherwise discovered. The ability of mathematics to describe nature provides science one of its most useful but mysterious tools. The capacity of rational thought to apprehend the laws of nature is usually taken for granted without comment, but many scientists have regarded this fact of life with awe.

Maxwell's equations predicted the velocity at which electromagnetic radiation travels in a vacuum. This number was too near the known speed of light to be a coincidence. Further, Maxwell's work showed that magnetic effects could self-propagate in a vacuum. The conclusions were obvious. Light is a visible type of electromagnetism. Maxwell's mathematical theory predicted other frequencies of radiation beyond the visible. These were all quickly discovered. William Herschel found that by passing a thermometer across a beam of light emerging from a prism, heating effects increased from yellow to red and increased still further beyond the red. The invisible radiation beyond red became known as infrared. Radiation below the violet at the other end of the prism was discovered by Johann Ritter and came to be called ultraviolet. Then Heinrich Hertz showed that electromagnetic radiation could travel from a transmitter to a receiver without wires or any physical connection. Hertz himself did not believe his electric waves would find any practical application. Tragically, he died at age 37 in 1894. Just six years later, Hertzian waves carrying an audible message were transmitted across the Atlantic Ocean. Hertz had discovered radio. A few years later, Wilhelm Roentgen stumbled onto another strange form of radiation which could pass through solid matter. Not knowing what to call them, he dubbed them "x-rays." Soon the entire spectrum of electromagnetism was in place and light was known to be a narrow band of electromagnetic wavelengths of visible frequency.

As the 19th century came to a close, most physicists were confident that the electromagnetic theory would provide the final word on the nature of light. In fact, the most eminent physicist in England, Lord Kelvin, stated that our knowledge of physics was just about complete. It was believed that all the important discoveries had been made. There remained but a few little puzzles to work out. These few "little puzzles," however, were destined to effectively topple the powerful edifice of classical, mechanistic physics forever. The stage was set for a whole new world.

A new century and the new physics both officially began in the same year. In 1900, Max Planck announced his "Quantum Theory" and a revolution was unleashed. The story is told of Planck that as an undergraduate he was advised against specializing in physics in favor of his other love, music; the reason given that physics was nearly a closed subject. Planck, however, did decide for physics and began work on one of those remaining "little puzzles" about light. The question he concentrated on involved what was technically known as black body radiation. Certain metal, such as an iron rod, will become self-luminous as it is heated to very high temperatures. At 3,000 degrees Celsius it glows "red hot"—i.e., gives off light of a wave frequency we see as red. At 6,000 degrees, it glows white hot. The problem was to mathematically calculate the color of the glow at different temperatures. According to the classical, Newtonian laws of thermodynamics, the light energy released should be in a continuous flow. This, however, was not the observed case. In order to match his mathematical formula to observed data, Planck was forced to introduce a "unit" of energy which he called a "quantum," designated by h in his formula $E = nhf$. Although the formula matched experiment, the implications were contrary to classical laws. If I can travel at 5 m.p.h. and at 6 m.p.h., then I should be able to travel at $5\frac{1}{2}$ mph and anywhere continuously in between. The radiation from the iron rod did not conform to this logical thinking but instead occurred in defined spurts only. Planck's h was the first hint that the classical laws of physics would fail at the atomic level. Now the question can be asked: just what is h and why does it exist? In one sense, it is precisely known what h is. It is this: .0000000000000000000000000065 erg-seconds. As for how and why it exists, we must content ourselves with accepting it as a fundamental feature of the universe.

Meanwhile, another little puzzle about light was being studied by an entirely unknown German Jew working as a patent clerk in Switzerland. The puzzle was the "photoelectric effect" and the stranger was Einstein. In 1905, Einstein suddenly appeared on the scene by publishing three papers in the German scientific journal *Annalen der Physik*. It was immediately recognized by a few discerning physicists that if Einstein's papers were proven true, he would become the Copernicus of the 20th century. However, two of these papers were so bizarre that it would take several years for the scientific community to take them seriously.

One of Einstein's papers was on the photoelectric effect. This effect was known but unexplained. When light shines on a metal surface, electrons are emitted by the metal causing an electric current to flow. (This effect is now brought to practical use in automatic doors.) Einstein's explanation of the photoelectric effect showed that light carried a fixed amount of energy, a "quantum of

light." In other words, he seemed to be reviving the particle theory of light which had long been laid to rest. In the
following years, more evidence for the quantum of light
became available. The name *photon* was eventually given
for a single particle of light. Physicists were forced to
accept the illogical dual nature of light which sometimes
manifests as waves, sometimes as particles.

Now we return to the double-slit experiment, this time
replacing the last screen with a piece of photographic film
and sending the light through the two slits *one photon at a
time*. Each individual photon passes through the double-
slit screen and leaves its single mark on the photographic
film. But as more and more photons are allowed to pass
one at a time and leave their single mark, the pattern of
wave interference still slowly emerges! If one slit is covered, the interference pattern does not build up. But when
both are opened, the interference pattern occurs. The
question is: how does a single photon know when the
second slit is opened and when it is closed? There is no
objective answer to this question. The old laws of mechanical physics cannot explain this aspect of light. At stake
here is the classical assumption that the objective world is
entirely self-explanatory without reference to any possible
higher dimensional order beyond our viewpoint here in
time-space. Scientists who have studied the double-slip
and certain comparable experiments admit they are
impossible to visualize or comprehend logically. Richard
Feynman, who won a Nobel Prize in physics in 1965, put it
this way: "I think it is safe to say that no one understands
quantum mechanics. Do not keep saying to yourself, if
you can possibly avoid it, 'but how can it be like that?'. . .
Nobody knows how it can be like that."[5] But however
bizarre it appears, quantum theory has been remarkably

---

[5]Richard Feynman, cited in *Quantum Reality* by Nick Herbert (New York:
Doubleday, 1985), p. xiii.

successful. It correctly predicted the behavior of micro-chips, photocells, lasers, nuclear reactors, and much other modern technology.

One more of Einstein's 1905 papers dealt with light. This was of course the famous Special Theory of Relativity proclaiming $E = mc^2$. With this paper, the nature of light lost any vestige of common sense. Einstein resolved the paradox of light's velocity which had first occurred to him at age 16 by concluding it is impossible to catch up with a beam of light. Its velocity cannot be considered velocity in the common sense of physical laws. Take a normal example of velocity such as a baseball traveling toward an outfielder at a certain speed, say 90 m.p.h. If the outfielder runs forward to catch it at 15 m.p.h., the ball hits his glove at the combined speed of 105 m.p.h.[6] Another "normal" illustration involves a person walking on a moving train. If the train is moving at 60 m.p.h. and the person walks in the same direction as the train is moving, at a speed of 1 m.p.h., he will be walking at 1 m.p.h. relative to his own frame of reference, but relative to a non-moving observer standing on solid ground outside the train, the walker's speed would be measured at 60 m.p.h. + 1 m.p.h. com-bined.[7] This is all quite reasonable. But Einstein claimed that light behaves quite differently and is completely inde-pendent of the motion of any observer. Consider the example of a spaceship traveling toward the sun at a very high speed: "If the passengers on the ship measure the velocity of the light coming from the sun, they will find that it passes them at 186,000 miles per second. If they turn the ship around and accelerate until it is speeding in the opposite direction, the light form the sun will still pass them at 186,000 m.p.s. Light seems to go no faster when

---

[6]Michael Sobel, *Light* (Chicago: University of Chicago Press, 1987), p. 204.
[7]Ben Bova, *The Beauty of Light* (New York: Wiley, 1988), p. 136.

they are rushing to meet it than when they are running away from it."[8]

In addition, no matter how fast the spaceship travels, it could never catch up to one particular ray of light. No matter how fast it pursued the light, the light would always be speeding away from the spaceship at 186,000 m.p.s. Thus, the speed of light is the absolute. What is relative is time and space. As the spaceship (or any object) approaches the speed of light, its mass increases and time slows down for anyone on board. When a spaceship travels away from the earth at a velocity 99 percent of the speed of light, the passengers would age only one year for every seven years that passed on earth.[9] A clock traveling at the speed of light would stop completely. Time stops at the speed of light.

Although such notions were (and still are) hard for people to accept, the theory of relativity has been confirmed experimentally over and over again in the last 85 years. The relativistic increase in mass has been confirmed in modern accelerators which are capable of bringing electrons up to a speed of more than 99.99999999 percent of the speed of light. The Relativistic slowing of time has been experimentally confirmed by flying atomic clocks in commercial aircraft. The clocks slow down by exactly the amount predicted by relativity theory.[10]

Scientists were now beginning to appreciate the fundamental role that light plays in the material universe. Its absolute and mysterious nature forms a bridge from the relative, objective world we see around us to that infinite realm beyond time-space. Light is the gossamer veil between this world and the next:

---

[8]Richard Morris, *Light*, pp. 162, 163.
[9]Richard Morris, *Light*, p. 163.
[10]Timothy Ferris, *Coming of Age in the Milky Way*, p. 192.

As nature's most subtle creation, the photon tee-
ters on a knife-edge. With rest mass equal to zero,
if it traveled the slightest bit slower than c, its
energy and mass would become zero. It would
have ceased to exist. Alternatively, if the photon
traveled at c but had a rest mass the slightest bit
greater than zero, it would have infinite energy
and, in effect, could never have been created. . . .
The quantization of light, along with the theory of
relativity, forces upon us a new perspective concerning this number we call c. It is no longer just
the speed of light but is an inborn characteristic of
the universe, of spacetime if you will; it is the
speed greater than which nothing can go. Within
space time are created, for reasons we do not
know, certain fundamental types of particles.
Each is defined by a small set of parameters, one
of which is rest mass. (Another is electric charge, a
third is intrinsic spin.) The photon is one, perhaps
the only one, with zero mass. Hence it may (and it
must) travel at c.[11]

Scientists (such as Niels Bohr and Ernest Rutherford) now
began putting together new explanations of how light
interacts with matter, bringing forth an entirely new
model of the atom. Far from being an indivisible block of
matter, as previously supposed, the atom was now
described as a unit of energy—electrons swirling around a
nucleus—capable of being broken apart into light. The
force of electromagnetism holds electrons in their orbits,
combines individual atoms into molecules, and holds molecules together to make objects. All matter can now quite
literally be described as frozen light.

11Michael Sobel, *Light*, p. 207.

According to quantum theory, when a photon (a single unit of light) strikes an atom, the photon's energy is absorbed by the atom and an electron is boosted to a higher orbit instantaneously, *"without having traversed the intervening space.* The orbital radii themselves are quantized, and the electron simply ceases to exist at one point, simultaneously appearing at another. This is the famously confounding 'quantum leap,' and it is no mere philosophical poser, unless it is taken seriously, the behavior of the atom cannot be predicted accurately."[12] When the electron returns to its former orbit it gives off a single photon. Thus light is created and destroyed in the mysterious quantum leap as matter comes into being.

The solidity of matter is now put into question. Is the physical world as substantial as it appears? The atom itself is certainly not solid. A single atom with its nucleus surrounded by swirling electrons has been likened by visual analogy to a nickel in the center of a large empty cathedral. The nickel symbolizes the nucleus, and the walls of the empty cathedral represent the outer path of the whirling electrons. Thus an atom is in actuality almost entirely empty space. The solid appearance of matter must now be considered more illusionary than real. As Amaury de Riencourt puts it in his recent book, *The Eye of Shiva*:

> The world we see and experience in everyday life is simply a convenient mirage attuned to our very limited senses, an illusion conjured by our perceptions and our mind. All that is around us (including our own bodies) which appears so substantial, is ultimately nothing but ephemeral networks of particle-waves, whirling around at lightning speed, colliding, rebounding, disintegrating in almost total emptiness — so-called matter is mostly

---

[12]Timothy Ferris, *Coming of Age in the Milky Way*, p. 288.

emptiness, porportionately as void as intergalactic space, void of anything except occasional dots and spots and scattered electric charges. For instance, any single one of the roughly 10^{27} atoms of the average human body is already minute enough — in decimal notation its average diameter of one or two Ångströms is about 0.0000000001 metre. Yet, although almost all of its mass is concentrated in the nucleus, the radius of this nucleus itself is one hundred thousand times smaller — so small, in fact, that if all the nuclei of all the atoms that make up the whole of mankind were packed tight together, their global aggregate would be the size of a large grain of rice! An atom, therefore, is almost completely empty space in which minute particles whirl around within its confines at speeds of up to forty thousand miles per second — enough to make us dizzy when we grasp the fact that, in the last resort, that is what our physical bodies and everything material are ultimately made of.[13]

The obvious question has been raised that if the submicroscopic world is nearly empty space, how is it, for example, that a table supports my elbow as I lean on it. Why do I not slide effortlessly through? The saving grace is the negative electric charge of the atoms' electrons which repel each other. Turn off this electricity, and the whole world would disappear.

As if the previous considerations were not yet mind-boggling enough, there remains one last enigmatic aspect of light which we must now consider. This subject concerns the property of quantum particles called *spin* and was at the center of a well-known disagreement between

---

[13]Amaury de Riencourt, *The Eye of Shiva* (New York: William Morrow, 1981), pp. 28, 29.

Einstein and his colleague Neils Bohr. The principles involved are much too technical to give a comprehensive description here, so a brief sketch will have to suffice. The principal facts, although this cursory analysis may render them unbelievable, are these: there is always a correlation in the spin of two quantum particles of light that have once been connected. When a measurement is taken on one particle, the twin particle is affected *instantaneously* even though it may be hundreds of thousands of miles away. Since no information signal can travel from one point in space to another faster than the speed of light, the instantaneous spin correlation seems to point to some kind of universal connection in a higher dimensional order.

Einstein and Bohr never came to a mutual agreement on this subject. The technology available during their lifetimes was inadequate to settle the issue. But in 1982, an experiment using light was performed in France which substantially verifies Bohr's view and points to a mysterious "non-local" connection between subatomic particles. The experiment was performed by Alain Aspect with two colleagues using photons produced by atoms of mercury vapor excited into a higher energy state with a laser beam. With the aid of switching mechanisms that operate in the billionths of a second, fast enough to catch a photon after it has left its source but before it travels more than a few yards away, Aspect and his group measured the spin of a stream of numerous paired photons. The correlations were far greater than accountable by the laws of classical physics.[14] This experiment supports the hypothesis of a higher dimensional order, a realm beyond time, space, and the speed of light.

The hypothesis of an ultimate basic reality in a higher dimensional order is considered by some physicists to be

---

[14]Michael Talbot, *Beyond the Quantum* (New York: Bantam, 1988), p. 32.

the culminating achievement of 20th-century physics. This basic reality has been given various names. The one most universally adopted is "the implicate order," proposed by one of today's top physicists, David Bohm. Bohm maintains that without reference to the implicate order, our theories of matter will remain incomplete. What is most interesting is that Bohm sees the implicate order as not only the essential ground of inanimate matter but of consciousness as well.

Bohm's views on consciousness are scientifically controversial, but by no means unique. In fact, a surprising number of 20th-century physicists have spoken out in favor of the concept of a universal consciousness originating outside time-space. Present-day physicist Bob Toben has called consciousness "the totality beyond space-time" and "the missing hidden variable in the structuring of matter."[15] Sir Arthur Eddington, who was knighted in 1930 for his contribution to physics and astronomy, held this opinion: "Recognising that the physical world is entirely abstract and without actuality apart from its linkage to consciousness, we restore consciousness to the fundamental position instead of representing it as an inessential complication occasionally found in the midst of inorganic nature at a late stage of evolutionary history. . . . If you take the view that the whole of consciousness is reflected in the dance of electrons in the brain, so that each emotion is a separate figure of the dance, then all features of consciousness alike lead into the external world of physics. But I assume that you have followed me in rejecting this view, and that you agree that consciousness as a whole is greater than those quasi-metrical aspects of it which are abstracted to compose the physical brain. . . . The idea of a universal Mind or Logos would be, I think, a fairly plausi-

---

[15]Bob Toben, *Space-time and Beyond: Toward an Explanation of the Unexplainable* (New York: Dutton, 1975), p. 11.

ble inference from the present state of scientific theory; at least it is in harmony with it."[16] James Jeans, who made fundamental contributions to the theory of electromagnetism and many other subjects, concurs: "When we view ourselves in space and time, our consciousnesses are obviously the separate individuals of a particle-picture, but when we pass beyond space and time, they may perhaps form ingredients of a single continuous stream of life. As it is with light and electricity, so it may be with life; the phenomena may be individuals carrying on separate existences in space and time, while in the deeper reality beyond space and time we may all be members of one body."[17]

David Bohm was recently interviewed on his ideas on the implicate order and specifically on the topic of light. This interview was conducted by Renée Weber as part of her efforts to describe the emerging correlations between religion and modern science. This interview is presented in Weber's recent book, *Dialogues with Scientists and Sages: The Search for Unity*. We conclude this chapter with segments of the Bohm/Weber conversation on light.

♦ ♦ ♦

WEBER There is one important idea that I would like to discuss and understand and that is the idea of light. That is especially important to me because you are a physicist. Light has been used as *the* privileged metaphor in the language of mysticism and experimental religions, going back to the Greeks and the East. In all these, light is the symbol of our union with the divine. They talk about a light without shadow, an all-suffusing light, and it comes

[16]Sir Arthur Eddington, *The Nature of the Physical World* (Ann Arbor, MI: University of Michigan Press, 1958), pp. 332, 323, 338.
[17]Sir James Jeans, *Physics and Philosophy* (New York, Macmillan, 1943), p. 204.

up as the central metaphor in near-death experiences. Do you have any hypothesis as to why light has been singled out as the privileged metaphor?

BOHM If you want to relate it to modern physics (light and more generally anything moving at the speed of light, which is called the null-velocity, meaning null distance), the connection might be as follows. As an object approaches the speed of light, according to relativity, its internal space and time change so that the clocks slow down relative to other speeds, and the distance is shortened. You would find that the two ends of the light ray would have no time between them and no distance, so they would represent immediate contact. (This was pointed out by G.N. Lewis, a physical chemist, in the 1920's.) You could also say that from the point of view of present field theory, the fundamental fields are those of very high energy in which mass can be neglected, which would be essentially moving at the speed of light. Mass is a phenomenon of connecting light rays which go back and forth, sort of freezing them into a pattern.

So matter, as it were, is condensed or frozen light. Light is not merely electromagnetic waves but in a sense other kinds of waves that go at that speed. Therefore all matter is a condensation of light into patterns moving back and forth at average speeds which are less than the speed of light. Even Einstein had some hint of that idea. You could say that when we come to light we are coming to the fundamental activity in which existence has its ground, or at least coming close to it.

WEBER Why is speed the determinant?

BOHM . . . We say that there is no speed at all at light. To call it speed is merely using ordinary language. In itself, when it is self-referential, there's no time, no space, no speed.

WEBER What is it?

BOHM It's just a primary conception. As you move faster and faster according to relativity your time rates slow down and the distance gets smaller, so as you approach very high speeds your own interval time and distance become less, and therefore if you were at the speed of light you could reach from one end of the universe to the other without changing your age at all.

WEBER Isn't that saying that it's approaching a timeless state?

BOHM That's right. We're saying that existentially speaking or logically speaking, time originates out of the timeless.

WEBER This is primary and time is derivative of it, cutting it down, freezing it, arresting it.

BOHM Yes, arresting it to a certain extent, not absolutely, but to a large extent.

WEBER When mystics use the visualization of light they don't use it only as a metaphor; to them it seems to be a reality. Have they tapped into matter and energy at a level where time is absent?

BOHM It may well be. That's one way of looking at it. As I've suggested the mind has two-dimensional and three-dimensional modes of operation. It may be able to operate directly in the depths of the implicate order where this [timeless state] is the primary actuality. Then we could see the ordinary actuality as a secondary structure that emerges as an overtone of the primary structure. . . .

WEBER For the mystics there is always light. The primary clear light in the *Tibetan Book of the Dead* is the first thing the dying person is aware of. If he doesn't move towards it or away from it or feel awe or fear or manipulate it in any way as if it were outside himself, then he merges with it and is liberated, *enlightened.* Christ says: "I am the light," and so on. I've always asked myself, why light? You're saying that from the point of view of a physicist, it has to do with the absence of speed and the closeness of contact.

BOHM Light is what enfolds all the universe as well. For example, if you're looking at this room, the whole room is enfolded into the light which enters the pupil of your eye and unfolds into the image and into your brain. Light in its generalized sense (not just ordinary light) is the means by which the entire universe unfolds into itself.

WEBER Is this a metaphor for you or an actual state?

BOHM It's an actuality. At least as far as physics is concerned.

WEBER Light is energy, of course.

BOHM It's energy and it's also information – content, form and structure. It's the potential of everything.

WEBER Physicists are not satisfied that they have understood light up to now because of the particle-wave paradox, right?

BOHM Yes, I think that to understand light we'll have to understand the structure underlying time and space more deeply. You can see that these issues are related in the sense that light transcends the present structure of time and space and we will never understand it properly in that present structure.

WEBER How would implicate order philosophy handle light?

BOHM It could handle it more naturally, mathematically speaking, because it doesn't commit itself to the idea of separate points in space; but it may say that the underlying reality is something which is not localized, and light is also something which is not localized. One view says that light moves from one place to another through a series of positions, and the other view says it doesn't do that at all. Rather, light exists; it just simply *is*.[18]

---

[18]Renee Weber, *Dialogues with Scientists and Sages: The Search for Unity* (London & New York: Routledge and Kegan Paul, 1986) pp. 44–47. Copyright © Renee Weber. Reproduced by permission of Penguin Books, Ltd.

14

THE LIGHT OF LIFE

It is the nature of matter itself, of pure, primordial substance. Substance dissolves into light. The only reason we do not notice it is the slowness of the decay. It is common enough as a metaphor, as a religious symbol. Dreamers have talked this way for ages. But according to grand unification it is not a dream. It is the literal and exact truth. We are composed of incipient radiance.

————George Greenstein
The Symbiotic Universe

The opening quotation is from the following source:

George Greenstein, *The Symbiotic Universe* (New York: William Morrow, 1988), p. 160.

◆ ◆ ◆

The opening verses of Genesis tell us that light was God's first work of creation. From that light, in six days, all of creation followed: the heavens, the earth, grass, fruit, birds, animals, and finally human beings. Science, too, has a creation account and it is remarkably similar, although modern cosmology has updated the "six days" to a more precise time scale: a great explosion of light began space-time 15 billion years ago in a Big Bang of electronuclear force; the first living cell on Earth evolved some 12 billion years later; and the first human, Homo erectus, appeared in China 1.8 million years before the present. Whether one prefers the biblical or the scientific version, it would appear that there exists a power in nature capable of taking the raw material of unbounded light and eventually coming up with us. If this is true, we might consider ourselves beings of light, in a way. As it turns out, we are indeed beings of light in a very literal way, as science is more and more discovering. Let's look at some of the modern discoveries of the light of the living body.

◆ ◆ ◆

Mechanistic biologists operate their craft under the assumption that both animate and inanimate matter will someday be completely explained by the known laws of chemistry and physics. Their approach denies any fundamental distinction between living and non-living systems other than the degree of complexity. They seek to define both life and consciousness as byproducts of highly organized matter.

On the other hand, many people who are not mechanistic biologists still insist on asking the question, "What is animating the living body?" These people find it more appropriate to view consciousness and life as spiritual, immaterial and fundamentally independent of matter. According to this view, life energy is not the result of organized matter, but in fact the organizing agent—mind is the maker.

The clash of viewpoints outlined above is known in science as the debate between mechanism versus vitalism. Mechanists do not believe in, nor do they seek to discover, a non-material essence of life. Vitalists, however, attempt to define the soul or spirit in a scientifically valid manner, proposing a large variety of names for the animating factor—life-energy, vital force, elan vital, bioplasm, orgone, odic force, to name a few. This energy is presumably restored to the body by the state of consciousness known as sleep, a universal but still completely unexplained phenomenon. The theories of vitalism run parallel to many schools of spirituality. In Taoism, the life energy is known as *chi*. It flows through the body along the acupuncture meridians. In Yoga, life energy is called *prana*. It pervades the entire physical body, constituting a second body known as the etheric body. This energy is a condensed form of the still more subtle energy of the soul— pure consciousness.

In the science of the early 20th century, mechanism had won a clear victory over vitalism. All the known data concerning life processes supported the view that life is a purely chemical phenomenon. A theory did exist within biology proposing electricity as the life-force, but the notion of bioelectricity was thought to be thoroughly disproved by experiment and it was generally considered a naive myth. But then, in the early 1960's, the idea that electricity played some role in living things gained new and convincing evidence, thanks to the salamander.

The salamander is a scaleless lizardlike animal with a peculiar talent called regeneration. If it loses a limb or its tail, it will simply grow a new one. This presented a great unsolved mystery for biologists. In 1960, a medical researcher named Dr. Robert Becker proposed to study regeneration in relation to electricity, citing new experiments measuring a current of electricity at the point of injury. He submitted his research proposal for funding and received this response: "We have a very grave basic concern over your proposal. This notion that electricity has anything to with living things was totally discredited some time ago. It has absolutely no validity, and the new scientific evidence you're citing is worthless. The whole idea was based on its appeal to quacks and the gullible public."[1]

Dr. Becker did finally receive funding for his project and began his experiments with salamanders and electricity. The results confirmed the importance of electromagnetism to life. Dr. Becker, as an orthopedist, later went on to successfully heal severe bone fractures with electric therapy. He then turned his attention to other aspects of bioelectricity and was able to detect electrical charges at some of the traditional acupuncture points.

The 1960's produced only a handful of published papers on bioelectricity; the data was slow to accumulate. The electromagnetic fields of the living body escaped detection, owing to their weakness and the overpowering constant presence of the earth's own electromagnetism. There simply were no instruments capable of making the measurement. But in 1964, a Nobel Prize went to the inventor of an electronic device which made it possible to build a field detector a thousand times more sensitive than any known before. This instrument is called a superconducting quantum interference device, or SQUID for short. Using this device and a shield to eliminate the interference of the earth's own electromagnetic fields, the fields of the heart, lungs, brain, etc., were finally precisely measured.

---

[1]Robert Becker and Gary Selden, *The Body Electric* (New York: William Morrow, 1985), p. 70.

A few years later, it was discovered that all living things emit actual light. Researchers in Germany and China detected the emission of coherent light from living cells. Their work was reported in *Cell Biophysics* and *Brain Mind Bulletin*: "The cells of living things give off coherent light—'biophotons'. . . . This light is different from what is known as bioluminescence, which we see in fireflies. Biophoton radiation ranges from infrared to ultraviolet. Growing cells radiate more intensely than fully developed ones. Dying cells also show intense photon emission."[2]

As science's instruments become increasingly refined, the life energy of the body is better understood. Today, some age-old vitalist theories have gained new credence. The fact that energy fields surround the body gives new support for the formerly ridiculed notion of the human aura. Clairvoyants have long claimed the ability to visualize an aura of light around living things. One modern-day seer has worked to define the aura in ways compatible with modern scientific understanding. She is Barbara Ann Brennan, a scientist and practicing healer. She worked for NASA at the Goddard Space Flight Center following the completion of her M.S. in Atmospheric Physics. She developed an interest in healing and psychotherapy and it was in the psychotherapeutic setting that she began to visualize auras, a lost talent she regained from her childhood. Brennan's scientific term for the aura is the "Human Energy Field," or HEF. "When I, as an adult, again began to see the life-energy fields, I became skeptical and confused. Of course, as a scientist I knew about energy fields, but they were impersonal and defined by mathematical formulae. Were they really there? Did they have meaning? Was I fabricating my experiences? Was it wishful thinking, or was I experiencing another dimension of reality that had meaning, was orderly and was very helpful in under-

---

2*Brain Mind Bulletin*, v. 10, no. 14, August 19, 1985, p. 1.

standing my present life circumstances and, in fact, life as a whole?

"There are many systems that people have created from their observations to define the auric field. All these systems divide the aura into layers and define the layers by locations, color, brightness, form, density, fluidity and function. I have observed seven layers during my work as a counselor and a healer. At first I could only see the lower layers, which are the most dense and easiest to see. The longer I worked, the more layers I could perceive. The higher the layer, the more expanded my consciousness needed to be to perceive it. My observations of the aura revealed to me an interesting dualistic field pattern. Every other layer of the field is highly structured, like standing waves of light patterns, while the layers in between appear to be composed of colored fluids in constant motion. These fluids flow through the form set by the shimmering standing light waves. The direction of flow is somewhat governed by the standing light form, since the fluid flows along the standing lines of light. The standing forms of light are themselves scintillating, as if they are composed of strings of many tiny, rapidly blinking lights, each blinking at a different rate. These standing light lines appear to have tiny charges moving along them.

"What I observed correlated with the many esoteric books written on the subject of the aura and energy fields. If we define the Human Energy Field as all fields or emanations from the human body, we can see that many well-known components of the HEF have been measured in the laboratory. These are the electrostatic, magnetic, electromagnetic, sonic, thermal and visual components of the HEF. All these measurements are consistent with normal physiological processes of the body and go beyond them to provide a vehicle for psychosomatic functioning. These studies show that the ordinary model of the body consisting of systems (like the digestive system) is insufficient.

An additional model based on the concept of an organizing energy field needs to be developed."[3]

The increasing understandings of the Human Energy Field may someday have a great impact on the healing arts, not only through auric healers, but in mainstream, allopathic medicine as well. Man-made electromagnetic fields are increasingly bombarding the environment. The effects of these fields are not clearly understood and may prove harmful. New studies show that there may indeed be cause for alarm. As reported in *World Research News*: "500,000 persons who are regularly exposed to strong electromagnetic fields had been examined in the state of Washington. 60% of them showed a higher rate of leukemia and 75% a higher rate of lymph gland cancer in comparison to a control group without such exposure."[4] But conversely, the healing potential of electromagnetism is also being explored. For example, light of a particular wavelength has been demonstrated to selectively kill cancer cells while remaining safe for normal tissue. Researchers at the Institute of Biophysics in Beijing, China successfully treated twenty-five cases of cancer (carcinomas of the oral cavity, skin, and cervix) using light therapy of a specific wavelength and density. They reported their findings in the scientific journal *Cancer*.[5]

The important role of light in bodily processes is matched by its effects on the mind. Brain wave activity is now easily measured by EEG and this activity has been shown to be highly sensitive to light stimulation. The

[3]Barbara Ann Brennan, *Hands of Light*, copyright © 1987 Barbara Ann Brennan (New York: Bantam Books, div. of Bantam Doubleday Dell Publishing Group, 1988), pp. 34, 37, 41, 42. Used by kind permission.
[4]*World Research News* (Sherman Oaks, CA: World Research Foundation, 3rd and 4th quarter, 1990), p. 7.
[5]Xu Yelin, et al, "The Selective Killing Effect of Special Wavelength Light in the Treatment of Human Superficial Cancer," *Cancer*, June 1, 1990, vol. 65, no. 11, pp. 2482–2487.

effects of light on a person's state of mind have been experienced from time immemorial as people have gazed into the flickering light of a fire. Science has taken this simple age-old technique of quieting the mind and brought it into the lab. Soon after EEG instruments first recorded the electrical activity of the brain in the 1920's, it was discovered that brain wave frequency is altered by light stimulation. This effect is known as *entrainment* — if a rhythmic flickering of light is flashed into a subject's eyes, the person's brain wave activity automatically resonates to that frequency. Brain waves are divided into four major rhythms: Beta, Alpha, Theta, and Delta. Beta waves are associated with normal waking consciousness. Alpha and Theta are increasingly relaxed states, and Delta waves indicate deep sleep. By flashing a light into a subject's eyes at the Theta frequency, that person's brain waves will soon drop to the same rate, thus producing states of deep reverie and meditation-like trances.

A current researcher of entrainment instruments described his own personal experience with one such device: "I turned the frequency dial downward, which caused the lights to flash more slowly, and watched the digits decrease through the teens and stop at 5 cycles per second — the slow theta waves that accompany deep reverie, meditation, and mental imagery. The brightness of the flashing lights increased. . . .I knew the tiny flashing lights were plain white, and yet the visions that appeared to me were vivid, spectacular, of bright primary colors — jagged alien landscapes, narrowing tunnels of swooping looping light, swirling multicolored checkerboards, a realistic view across the gray surface of a pond being stippled into fragmental light patterns by a gentle rainfall, sleek fish moving below the surface. I felt my attention drawn irresistibly inward. My tension was melting away. I was aware there were people in the room, but it was of no interest — they were in another world, far away. I experimented with different frequencies and patterns of stimulation, and with each twist of the dials the visions would change. I noticed that some visions would call up vivid memories. I dialed back to the pond, and suddenly I was a kid again, stalking frogs, feeling the sun hot on the back of my neck, smelling the green algae and mud of the pond."[6]

The effects of light on body and mind continue to pose a great and wonderful mystery. But there are indications that someday these forces will be within our understanding and control. The seemingly superhuman powers attained by some accomplished yogis attest to the fact that there is much still to learn about the human body and its potential. By bringing yogis and their powers under scientific scrutiny, important knowledge will surely be gained. One modern yogi, Swami Rama from Rishikish, India, has demonstrated his powers for studies conducted at the Menninger Foundation in Topeka, Kansas. He is able to self-regulate bodily functions beyond normal control by manipulating the "prana," as he calls it, the life-energy. In 1971, an experiment was conducted in which the yogi was able to stop the beating of his heart. Elmer Green, the conductor of the experiment describes the event:

> Our study in 1971 of Swami Rama, a yogi from Rishikesh, India, produced a few self-regulation events in the lab which Rama said represented energy control. Before he put his heart into a state of atrial flutter Rama turned to Alyce, on her way to the lab's control room, and said, "When my heart stops, call over the intercom and say, 'That's all.' " When I asked why he wanted that, he said, "Since I am not prepared in the usual way for this experiment (having not fasted for three days), I do

---

[6]Michael Hutchinson, *Megabrain* (New York: William Morrow, 1986), p. 26.

not want to do it too long . . . I do not want to take a chance on damaging my subtle heart."

It took further discussion over a period of days to define "subtle heart," but in the swami's mind (as in Patanjali's *Yoga Sutras*) the human is an energy structure of which the "densest part" is the physical body. As the physical magnet is the densest section of a magnetic field, so the structure of the physical heart is the densest section of a subtle (energy structure) heart.

When I asked Swami how he managed to put his heart into the peculiar non-pumping state of atrial flutter, he said that a large energy center in the middle of his chest (the "heart chakra in the subtle body") was connected by a little line of "light" (prana) to a small energy center (chakra) associated with the right ear. In a state of meditation he "looked" inside himself, and when he saw the line of light he made it become "very bright," and then the heart "stopped."

A few months later, at a meeting of neurologists for whom I was speaking on biofeedback and yoga, I was pressed by one questioner to explain how the Swami did that "trick." As a psycho-social experiment, I decided to give the Swami's own explanation. After that there was a long silence. Then one of the physicians stood up and gave a neurological interpretation. There is a loop of the vagus nerve (which controls the heart) very close to the right ear; the Swami obviously had learned a way to manipulate it. "Isn't it interesting," the doctor said, "the Swami has developed a metaphor (a visualization, please note) which when thought about is able to manipulate the vagus nerve!"

I did not say it, but I thought, "Who really has the metaphor, the doctor or the Swami?" Are we in fact looking at a many-dimensioned cosmos of energy fields with our space-time brains, and seeing a three-dimensional slice which we call physical matter?[7]

Today, science has peeked beyond the material solid appearance of things. We know ourselves as children of light, no longer by virtue of spiritual understanding alone, but through scientific endeavor. The goal of science and religion is the same, the discovery of truth. As each system proceeds in this pursuit, they surely must come together. So, too, must body and spirit harmonize. Enlightenment is not a spiritual victory gained at the expense of the physical body; rather, body, mind and spirit are one. We end this chapter with the words of one of today's spiritual sages, Da Love Ananda, who teaches that inherent in the body are all the functions necessary for expanded consciousness and knowledge of the inner light.

The structure of the manifest, mortal, and always changing body-mind is demonstrated as a range of functional possibility extended between two extremes—the higher brain and the lower body. This range between extremes or polar opposites corresponds to the subtler energy structure that envelops the soul in its association with the phenomenal realms. Thus, both the soul in its subtle energy field and the extended or Radiated body-

---

[7]Stanislov Grof, *Ancient Wisdom and Modern Science* (New York: State University of New York Press, copyright © 1984), pp. 249, 250. Used by kind permission.

mind that expresses the soul and its energy field are structures in a bipolar form, with subtler processes apparent above, and grosser processes apparent below.

The soul is only temporarily, and without ultimate necessity, associated with particular psychophysical states—the result of tendencies acquired through past associations with conditional states of experience that are less than Perfect Contemplation of the Divine Condition.

For this reason, the soul, which is Pure Consciousness and Eternal Life, identifies with the "I," the self-reference of the psycho-physical being. And the embodied or self-limited existence of the soul thus becomes a struggle of experience, and possible growth, by virtue of fixed and automatic association with the born body-mind.

The "Kingdom of God" is a matter of the literal Translation of the whole bodily being of the individual into the unqualified and All-Pervading Light of the World. That Light is not in objective or subjective relationship to us. It is the Light or Radiance we intuit to be the Condition of our very existence and consciousness. We must each become a living, single, or whole body sacrifice, through love and esoteric practice, into the Radiance wherein we have arisen.

The Light of God and the Light of the soul are One. It is Perfect Radiance, or White Brightness. All manifest forms are parts of a universe or total spectrum of modifications or solidifications of the range of possibility inherent in Original Light, or Radiance. Thus, the soul in its casing of spectral energies is expressed as a range of colors, from red and golden yellow at its lowest point or pole to violet and blue at its highest point or pole.

The Enlightenment of the whole and entire body-mind is a matter of the Transcendental Infusion of the body-mind with the unqualified Radiance of the Heart. This is done by a process in which that Radiance first pervades the entire brain, to its extreme, and then, via the brain, invades all the rest of the extended body-mind. The Current of Radiance is permitted to pervade and "unlock" every cell of the body and to dissolve every thought or image that makes the mind. And the life-Current is established in perfect polarization, toe to crown, so that the mechanical motions toward psycho-physical experience are dissolved in the Divine Radiance, prior to all independent experience.

The Heart, or Awakened Consciousness, prior to the reflexive gestures of attention, self, and experience, is the Truth of the body-mind of Man. And when Man Awakens to the Truth of the Heart, then even the World, the Totality of Experience, Dissolves in Truth. Thus, in the Way of Radical Intuition, the Heart is Awake, with "open eyes." The Heart does not turn in on Itself or away as Itself. Rather, It is Awake as Itself, and totally Aware.[8]

---

[8]Da Avabhasa, aka Da Love Ananda, *The Enlightenment of the Whole Body*, copyright © 1978 The Free Daist Communion (Lower Lake, CA: The Dawn Horse Press, 1978), pp. 460, 490, 514. Used by kind permission.

15

THE LIGHT OF DEATH

At that point, I had no consciousness anymore of having a body. It was just pure consciousness. And this enormously bright light seemed almost to cradle me. I just seemed to exist in it and be part of it and be nurtured by it and the feeling just became more and more and more ecstatic and glorious and perfect.

————from a Near-Death Experience

◆ ◆ ◆

We now come full circle and again ponder the forbidden question posed by Nachiketa four thousand years ago. Young Nachiketa, as legendary hero, was able to penetrate the veil between this world and the next and learn the secret of life after death. Similar tales abound in the folklore of every subsequent age and culture, but it is our own age which contributes to this tradition most prolifically. The modern abundance of life after death accounts is due not to a spiritual advancement, but to science. Modern medical technology has made it possible to literally bring a person back to life after he or she has been clinically dead without breath or pulse for several minutes. In some instances, people retain a recollection of their experiences while "dead." Such occurrences are on the increase today and the phenomenon is widely known and vigorously studied. The event is called a near-death experience, or NDE, a term first coined by Raymond Moody in 1975 and now a household word. The ongoing research has revealed several common elements of the NDE, the greatest of which is the encounter with a being of light at the end of a tunnel. The being of light is typically described by the near-death experiencer as ineffably warm, beautiful and loving, and often identified as Christ or some other religious figure. Following is a collection of being-of-light accounts gathered from one of the major new books on the subject, *Heading Toward Omega* by Kenneth Ring.

◆ ◆ ◆

In 1956, a young man of 14 was traveling with his family from Texas to Mississippi. The car in which he was riding was caught in a flash flood and the young man was trapped and submerged for a time, nearly drowning . . .

I knew I was either dead or going to die. But then something happened. It was so immense, so powerful that I gave up on my life to see what it was. I wanted to venture into this experience, which started as a drifting into what I could only describe as a long tunnel of light. But it wasn't just a light, it was a protective passage of energy with an intense brightness at the end which I wanted to look into, to touch. There were no sounds of any earthly thing. Only the sounds of serenity, of a strange music like I had never heard. A soothing symphony of indescribable beauty blended with the light I was approaching.

I gave up on life. I left it behind for this new wonderful thing. I did not want to go back to life. For what I knew was that what lay ahead was to be so wondrous and beautiful that nothing should stop me from reaching it.

As I reached the source of the light I could see in. I cannot begin to describe in human terms the feeling I had at what I saw. It was a giant infinite world of calm, and love, and energy and beauty. It was as though human life was unimportant compared to this. And yet it urged the importance of life at the same time it solicited death as a means to a better, different life. It was all being, all beauty, all meaning for existence. It was all the energy of the universe forever in one immensurable place.

In April 1977, while raking leaves in front of his house, a man in his 50s suffered a heart attack. . .

A brilliant white-yellow warm pillar of light confronted me. I was now in a light golden cellular embodiment and the greatest feeling of warmth and love and tenderness became part of me. My consciousness or soul was at the foot or base. When I tried to look up (not exactly so, but the closest words I can use) I saw the sweet smile and love of my father at the time when I was a young child and he held me and loved me. I felt this love permeating my being. (I had never any conscious remembrance of this nor thought of my father for years.)

Instantly my entire life was laid bare and open to this wonderful presence, "GOD." I felt inside my being his forgiveness for the things in my life I was ashamed of, as though they were not of great importance. I was asked—but there were no words; it was a straight mental instantaneous communication—"What had I done to benefit or advance the human race?" At the same time all my life was presented instantly in front of me and I was shown or made to understand what counted. I am not going into this any further but, believe me, what I had counted in life as unimportant was my salvation and what I thought was important was nil.

In September 1971, a young man was talking to a friend on the phone during an electrical storm. When lightning struck his house, he was electrocuted and was without pulse or respiration for nine minutes. He was resuscitated but suffers some permanent neurological damage and muscle degeneration . . .

. . . as the light came toward me, it came to be a person—yet it wasn't a person. It was a being that radiated. And inside this radiant luminous light which had a silver tint to it—white, with a silver tint to it—[was] what looked to be a man. . . .

Now, I didn't know exactly who this was, you know, but it was the first person that showed up and I had this feeling that the closer this light got to me, the more awesome and the more pure this love—this feeling that I would call love. . . . And this person said, "Do you know where you are?" I never got a chance to answer that question, for all of a sudden—quote, unquote—"my life passed before me." But it was not my life that passed before me nor was it a three-dimensional carica- ture of the events in my life. What occurred was every emotion I have ever felt in my life, I felt. And my eyes were showing me the basis of how that emotion affected my life. What my life had done so far to affect other people's lives using the feeling of pure love that was surrounding me as the point of comparison. And I had done a terrible job. God! I mean it. You know, I'd done a horrible job, using love as the point of comparison. . . . Lookin' at yourself from the point of how much love you have spread to other people is devas- tatin'. You will never get over it.

In 1952, a woman was giving birth to her second child, when . . .

. . . the next thing I knew, I was in—I was standing in a mist and I knew *immediately* that I had died and I was so happy that I had died but I was still alive. And I cannot tell you how I *felt*. It was, "Oh, God, I'm dead, but I'm here! I'm me!" And I started pouring out these enormous feelings of gratitude. . . . My consciousness was filled with nothing but these feelings of gratitude because I still existed and yet I knew perfectly well that I had died. . . .

While I was pouring out these feelings . . . the mist started being infiltrated with enormous light and the light just got brighter and brighter and brighter and, it is so bright but it doesn't hurt your eyes, but it's brighter than anything you've ever encountered in your whole life. At that point, I had no consciousness anymore of having a body. It was just pure consciousness. And this enormously bright light seemed almost to cradle me. I just seemed to exist in it and be part of it and be nurtured by it and the feeling just became more and more and more ecstatic and glorious and perfect. And everything about it was—if you took the one thousand best things that ever happened to you in your life and multiplied by a million, maybe you could get close to this feeling, I don't know. But you're just engulfed by it and you begin to know a lot of things.

I remember I knew that everything, everywhere in the universe was OK, that the plan was perfect. That whatever was happening—the wars, famine, whatever—was OK. Everything was perfect. Somehow it was all a part of the perfection, that we didn't have to be concerned about it at all. And the whole time I was in this state, it seemed infinite. It was timeless. I was just an infinite being in perfection. And love and safety and security and knowing that nothing could happen to you and you're home forever. That you're safe forever. And that everybody else was.

The next account is another childbirth incident.

I was 22 years old, delivering my second child, a little girl. The date was June 18, 1954. I began to hemorrhage badly (I'm told) but I recall a great pain in my chest that was making it impossible for me to draw in more air after exhaling. I recall a sense of being pulled (up!—not down) by some great force, out of the room toward a bright light which seemed far away at first but I "flew" toward it very swiftly. The pain fell behind me like ribbons or streamers trailing me, as I "knew" I was going faster and faster. The "light" appeared to be a window of some kind and I was momentarily alarmed that I would be hurt as I crashed into it, because I could not possibly stop myself in time at such high speed. I automatically shut my eyes and braced myself for the "crash" which was unavoidable (I thought).

Nothing crashed. I suddenly stopped and felt myself lying perfectly still—like floating on water. My sense of belonging, love, peace, and well-being was (as they all say) indescribable. It was absolute—perfect—wonderful. I didn't know where I was, but I didn't care, I would be content to stay there *forever*! I was alone, but *not* lonely. Even though there was no visual means of determining my position in this environment of "nothing," I "knew" I was lying down—rather than standing up.

Then I received the knowledge (no one was there with me and no one spoke, as we speak) that I was to wait there until a person came to talk to me. Then, I "knew" he was on his way toward me from an unthinkable distance away. He (rather than a "she") came to me at an unthinkable high speed, passing through the universe, through whole galaxies to come to where I was. I was in a world (a huge world) of total nothingness, except myself. The bright light I had seen at first, as a window in a world of total darkness, was all about me now, but not bright anymore—soft now, and soothing—or perhaps no light at all (and) no darkness either. More a haze. I felt so very, very comfortable there.

I "sensed" this person's approach toward me, and I "knew" the exact instant he entered into the outer edge of the world (or state of awareness?) I was in. He came to me from my right-hand side. In a matter of seconds he entered "my world" hundreds and thousands of light years away (the edge of it, I mean) and travelled to my side (he was standing) and took hold of my right hand.

When he took hold of my hand, I immediately knew him to be the greatest friend I had. I also knew that *I* was a very special person to him. The thrill of this touch of hands exceeds anything I have ever experienced on earth, in life as we know it. Our meeting was "understood"—"sensed"—not visual.

In May 1978, a 33-year-old man was working under his truck when its supports gave way and it fell on him. Paramedics were summoned by his son.

Then all this time, the speed is increasing. . . . Gradually, you realize . . . you're going [at] at least the speed of light. It might possibly be the speed of light or possibly even faster than the speed of light. You do realize that you're going just so fast and you're covering vast, vast distances in just hundredths of a second. . . .

And then gradually you realize that way, way off in the distance—again, unmeasurable distance—it

appears that it might be the end of the tunnel.
And all you can see is a white light. . . . And again,
remember that you are traveling at extreme speed.
[But] this whole process only takes . . . [say] one
minute and again emphasizing that you might
have traveled to infinity, just an unlimited number
of miles.

You then realize that you are coming to the end of
this tunnel and that this light is not just a brilliance
from whatever is at the end of the tunnel—it's an
extremely brilliant light. It's pure white. It's just so
brilliant. . . .

And then, before you is this—excuse me [he
pauses here]—is this most magnificent, just gor-
geous, beautiful, bright, white or blue-white light
[another pause]. It is so bright, it is *brighter* than a
light that would immediately blind you, but this
absolutely does not hurt your eyes at all. . . . It is so
bright, so brilliant, and so beautiful, but it doesn't
hurt your eyes. And the next series of events take
place—oh, within a millisecond, they take place—
more or less all at once, but of course in describing
them I'll have to take them one at a time.

The next sensation is this wonderful, wonderful
feeling of this light. . . . It's almost like a person. It
is *not* a person, but it is a being of some kind. It is a
mass of energy. It doesn't have a character like you
would describe another person, but it has a character in that it is more than just a thing. It is something to communicate to and acknowledge. And
also in size, it just covers the entire vista before
you. And it totally engulfs whatever the horizon
might be. . . .

Then the light immediately communicates to you. . . . This communication is what you might call telepathic. It's absolutely instant, absolutely clear. It wouldn't even matter if a different language was being spoken . . . whatever you thought and attempted to speak, it would be instant and absolutely clear. There would never be a doubtful statement made.

The first thing you're told is, "Relax, everything is beautiful, everything is OK." . . . You're immediately put at absolute ease. It's the most comfortable feeling that you could ever imagine. You have a feeling of absolute, pure love. It's the warmest feeling. [But] make sure you don't confuse it with warm in temperature, because there's no temperature involved. Whatever your senses would feel absolute perfect—if it's temperature, it's a perfect temperature. If it's either an exciting emotion or a placid emotion, it's just perfect and you feel this and you sense this. And it's so *absolutely* vivid and clear.

Then the thing is, the light communicates to you and for the first time in your life . . . [there] is a feeling of true, pure love. It can't be compared to the love of your wife, the love of your children, or some people consider a very intense sexual experience as love and they consider [it] possibly the most beautiful moment in their life—and it couldn't even begin to compare. All of these wonderful, wonderful feelings combined could not possibly compare to the *feeling*, the true love. If you can imagine what pure love would be, this would be the feeling that you'd get from this brilliant white light.

The second most magnificent experience . . . is you realize that you are suddenly in communications with absolute, total knowledge. It's hard to describe. . . . You can think of a question . . . and *immediately* know the answer to it. As simple as that. And it can be any question whatsoever. It can be on any subject. It can be on a subject that you don't know anything about, that you are not in the proper position even to understand and the light will give you the instantaneous correct answer and make you understand it. . . .

Needless to say, I had many questions answered, many pieces of information given to me, some of which is very personal, some of which is religiously orientated . . . one of the religious-orientated questions was in regards to an afterlife and this was definitely answered through the experience itself. . . . There's absolutely no question in my mind that the light is the answer. Upon entering that light . . . the atmosphere, the energy, it's total pure energy, it's total knowledge, it's total love, pure love—everything about it is definitely the afterlife, if you will.

As a result of that [experience], I have very little apprehension about dying my natural death . . . because if death is anything, anything at all like what I experienced, it's gotta be the most wonderful thing to look forward to, absolutely the most wonderful thing.

In November 1970, an author-publisher collapsed during a hostile business meeting.

I was not aware of any of the activity going on in the room because where I was and what I was experiencing was not of this world. The last thing I remembered was that I prayed to God. Then another consciousness slowly began to unfold. It could have happened in seconds, in minutes, in years, or even in an eternity.

At first I became aware of beautiful colors which were all the colors of the rainbow. They were magnified in crystallized light and beamed with a brilliance in every direction. It was as if all this light was coming at me through a prism made by a most beautiful and purified diamond, and yet at the same time it was as if I were in its center. I was in a heavenly pasture with flowers. It was another place, another time, and perhaps it was even another universe. But it was definitely another consciousness—vibrant and more alive than the one I had known in my earthly life. My ears were filled with a music so beautiful no composer could ever duplicate it. It too was not of this world. It was soothing, gentle, and warm and seemed to come from a source deep within me.

Everything that occurred to me while I was in this state of conscious[ness] was vastly beyond anything I had ever experienced and yet at the same time it was familiar—as if I had always known of its existence. Even now when I try to describe something so beautiful I am mute with awe. There are no words in any language to describe such grandeur. Even the great literary works by men and women fortunate enough to have experienced this blissful state only paint a shadow of its glory. I don't know to this day where I was, I was no longer aware of my physical existence on earth, of my friends, my family, or my relatives. I was in a

state that existed of nothing more than consciousness, but what a sublime consciousness it was! It
was like a rebirth into another, higher kind of life.

As my senses expanded I became aware of colors
that were far beyond the spectrum of the rainbow
known to the human eye. My awareness stretched
out in all three hundred sixty degrees. It was as if I
was in the center of a lotus flower which was
unfolding its beauty around me in every direction.
I became aware of being in the middle of a tunnel.
I was speeding closer and closer to a light at the
other end. In the far distance I saw what I can only
describe in the limited language available to me
now, as two circles.

In the middle of one circle was a most beautiful
being. It was neither a man nor a woman, but it
was both. I have never, before or since, seen anything as beautiful, loving, and perfectly pleasant
as this being. An immense, radiant love poured
from it. An incredible light shone through every
single pore of its face. The colors of the light were
magnificent, vibrant and alive. The light radiated
outward. It was a brilliant white superimposed
with what I can only describe as a golden hue. I
was filled with an intense feeling of joy and awe. I
was consumed with an absolutely inexpressible
amount of love. I had the overpowering feeling
that I was in the presence of the source of my life
and perhaps even my creator. In spite of the tre-
mendous awe it inspired, I felt I knew this being
extremely well. With all my heart I wanted to
embrace and melt into it as if we were one—for
although it was neither my mother nor my father,
it was both.

The second circle surrounded the first. In it I became aware of six shimmering mother-of-pearl-like impressions which unfolded and opened up in the way the petals of a freshly created flower open up to the sun. They were living beings. Their beauty, charm, splendid emanating colors, and the closeness I felt to them were breathtaking. From beyond this impression, I became aware of the most powerful, radiant, brilliant white light. It totally absorbed my consciousness. It shone through this glorious scene like the sun rising on the horizon through a veil which had suddenly opened. This magnificent light seemed to be pouring through a brilliant crystal. It seemed to radiate from the very center of the consciousness I was in and to shine out in every direction through the infinite expanses of the universe. I became aware that it was part of all living things and that at the same time all living things were part of it. I knew it was omnipotent, that it represented infinite divine love. It was as if my heart wanted to leap out of my body towards it. It was almost as though I had met my Maker. Even though the light seemed thousands and thousands of time stronger than the brightest sunlight, it did not bother my eyes. My only desire was to have more and more of it and to bathe in it forever.

Epilogue

This is the only method to bridge the gulf at present yawning between science and religion, between warring political ambitions and ideologies, between religious faiths, race, nations, classes and finally between men. This is the immortal light, held aloft by nature from time immemorial to guide the faltering footsteps of erring humanity across the winding path of evolution, the light which shone in the prophets and sages of antiquity, which continues to shine in the men of genius and seers of today, and will continue to shine for all eternity.

———Gopi Krishna
Kundalini, the Evolutionary Energy in Man